Kierkegaard and the Dialectics of Modernism

American University Studies

Series III
Comparative Literature

Vol. 19

PETER LANG
New York · Berne · Frankfurt am Main

Jørgen S. Veisland

Kierkegaard and the Dialectics of Modernism

PETER LANG
New York · Berne · Frankfurt am Main

Library of Congress Cataloging in Publication Data

Veisland, Jørgen S.,
    Kierkegaard and the Dialectics of Modernism.

    (American University Studies. Series III,
Comparative Literature; vol. 19)
    Bibliography: p.
    1. Kierkegaard, Søren, 1813-1855 – Influence.
2. Modernism (Literature) 3. Philosophy, Modern – 20th
Century. 4. Modernism (Aesthetics) I. Title.
II. Series: American University Studies. Series III,
Comparative Literature; v. 19.
B4377.V38   1985   809'.91   85-5595
ISBN 0-8204-0251-6
ISSN 0724-1445

CIP-Kurztitelaufnahme der Deutschen Bibliothek

Veisland, Jørgen S.:
Kierkegaard and the Dialectics of Modernism /
Jørgen S. Veisland. – New York; Berne;
Frankfurt am Main: Lang, 1985.
    (American University Studies: Ser. 3, Comparative
Literature; Vol. 19)
    ISBN 0-8204-0251-6

NE: American University Studies / 03

© Peter Lang Publishing, Inc., New York 1985

All rights reserved.
Reprint or reproduction, even partially, in all forms such as
microfilm, xerography, microfiche, microcard, offset prohibited.

Printed by Lang Druck, Inc., Liebefeld/Berne (Switzerland)

TABLE OF CONTENTS

PREFACE	i
INTRODUCTION: KIERKEGAARD'S PHILOSOPHY AND THE IDEOLOGY OF MODERNISM	1
CHAPTER 1: FREEDOM AND COMMUNICATION ACCORDING TO KIERKEGAARD	40
A. The Concept of Anxiety	40
B. The Seducer	55
C. Irony and Humor	65
CHAPTER 2: SEXUALITY AND COMMUNICATION ACCORDING TO FREUD	78
A. The Libido Theory	78
B. The Life and Death Instincts	82
C. Distorted Communication	99
CHAPTER 3: HERMENEUTICS AND THE CREATIVE PROCESS - HUNGER	107
CHAPTER 4: THE AESTHETICS OF REPETITION - A PORTRAIT, ULYSSES, HAVOC	148
CHAPTER 5: EROS AND TIME - AS I LAY DYING, THE DWARF, THE LIAR	202
CONCLUSION: THE POLITICAL EROS OF FORM AND BEAUTY	241
BIBLIOGRAPHY	249

PREFACE

The philosophy of Søren Kierkegaard is usually associated with Existentialism. A comprehensive study of the works of the Danish philosopher convinced me that there is also a profound and surprisingly close relationship between his ideas and Modernist philosophy and aesthetics. My book explores and elucidates this relationship by interpreting a number of English, American, and Scandinavian 20th century novels.

Quotations from works by Scandinavian authors are given in translation. Where I have used my own translation I have marked this with (J.V.).

I wish to thank the Danish Research Council for the Humanities, Copenhagen, Denmark, for its generous financial support which helped me complete this book.

Jørgen S. Veisland

Southwest China Teacher's University
January 15, 1985

INTRODUCTION

KIERKEGAARD'S PHILOSOPHY AND THE
IDEOLOGY OF MODERNISM

In *The Meaning of Contemporary Realism*, Georg Lukacs distinguishes between two main trends in contemporary literature, traditional realism and modernist anti-realism. Lukacs' analysis is consistent with his view of history as being something dynamic, changing, developing; his interpretation of anti-realism accords with the basic thesis of Marxist aesthetics and dialectical materialism, namely that there is a definite connection between art and the material base, between art and the totality of the relations of production, that art changes as production relations change, and that the only progressive art is the art of an ascending class, an art which expresses the consciousness of this class.

The dynamics of change are thus the foundation of Lukacs' critical perspective, and this perspective is rooted in the dialectics of Hegel and Marx; Hegelian and Marxian dialectics evolve as an interpretation of the subject-object relationship, an analysis of the interaction between individual and social environment. This interaction is the dynamic force behind change, and since social history reflects change, literature should also reflect it; the narrative structure of the novel, the novel form itself, must contain formal principles which determine and describe the development of growth of the protagonist through his interaction with the environment. Such principles inform the traditional realistic novel, as for example the 19th century Bildungsroman, whose hero undergoes changes through the impact of the environment on him and his impact on that same environment. This hero, furthermore, is autonomous, acting upon life and experience through a sense of identity and following a pattern of continuity. The hero of the "novel of education" thus creates a social and psychological dynamic which transforms him and his world. This realistic novel derives its central philosophy from the Aristotelian dictum that man is a social animal. In the traditional epic, Lukacs states, individual existence or ontological being, "cannot be distinguished from . . . social and historical environment"[1] - individual and social context create an inseparable unity.

The ontological concept which underlies the form, content, and the presentation of character in the modernist novel is contrary to the view of man as a social animal. Modernism depicts man in total isolation from his environment; man is seen to be solitary by nature, unable to establish meaningful relationships with others. In Joyce's Ulysses, for example, individual identity is not created through change, but suspended, or attenuated, in a web of memory- and sense-data, an intricate stream-of-consciousness, which - despite its pretended intention to express the simultaneity of past and present - produces a narrative style that depicts memory and retrospection. The characters of *Ulysses* meet and interact through memory, reflection, and dream only, and they exist in a medium of flux, the opposite of actual change. Flux is static, not dynamic, because the view of time underlying the narrative style of stream-of-consciousness is that of internal or psychological time, time divorced from historical time, or the real time of the objective world.

The solitary world of dream and subjective consciousness is elevated to a "universal condition humaine".[2] Lukacs draws attention to Heidegger's concept of man's "thrownness-into-being," and he sees this concept as the primary ideology of Modernism; according to this ontological concept, man is constitutionally unable to relate to others. In Modernism, man is conceived as an ahistorical being, according to Lukacs, and the negation of history creates the illusion of man as being confined within his own subjective consciousness; and that subjective consciousness is without a personal history - it is thrown into being. The prevailing illusion created by Modernism, then, is that <u>ahistoricity</u> has an ontological basis in the constitutional structure of the individual.

Contrary to Lukacs I suspect, however, that the authorial consciousness, or textual subject, in the modernist novel, may diverge from this ahistorical ontology; the author's intent in creating the illusion of a subjective, asocial consciousness coincides with an intent to create ironic distance; the narrative perspective departs from the point of view of the central character and points to the presence of a dual consciousness in Modernism, a dialectic between narrator and protagonist, with the narrator's perspective and mode of consciousness being inserted or injected into the novel. Thus, the form of modern consciousness depicted in Modernism is endowed with a self-reflective dialogue intended to demystify the illusory world of the subject and restore meaning to the world of the protagonist. In other words: the partially obscure content of subjective consciousness is elevated into awareness through the process of making the mind of the protagonist gradually coincide with the narrative consciousness. Irony, then, is used to bridge the gap between character and narrator; irony becomes a mediator in this process.

This dual level in Modernism is not due to a Marxian or Hegelian dialectic between subject and object; it is the dialogue of the subject with itself, the dialogue between the narrator and his text. I concede to the fact that Modernism is monadic by nature; that is, I agree that Modernism functions, through its imagery and its presentation of character, as a closed, subjective universe, but the consciousness inhabiting that universe is aware of an outside world. The intent of narrative consciousness in the modernist novel is not to negate the external world entirely, as Lukacs will have it, but to create a system of narrator-character interaction by which the consciousness of the protagonist approximates the higher level of consciousness inserted by the narrator or implied author. The tendency of the modern protagonist to approach and perhaps exceed the limits of his own intra-fictional experience is indicated, sometimes, by the fact that the author uses an extra-fictional framework through which he makes the reader aware of the distance the protagonist has to travel in order to attain the higher level of awareness. This higher knowledge, or pre-knowledge, can be a negative one, as in the preface to Tom Kristensen's novel <u>Havoc</u> where the author warns us not to cultivate the soul; cultivating the soul, i.e., staying within the limits of subjective consciousness, retreating further and further from the outside world, is precisely what the protagonist attempts to do, and the warning is not heeded till the end when the protagonist has discovered the truth expressed in the preface; the discovery by the protagonist that his "soul" is static and demonically bound in a pattern of psychic fixations from which he cannot liberate himself is a necessary process of cognition that must be undergone; this process of cognition is not only a demystification of illusion, it is also a prelude to the restoration of meaning, perhaps at an extra-fictional level. The novel <u>Havoc</u> is an example of an author using the literary medium to write himself out of an experience in order to start a new one. This writing oneself out of an experience can be interpreted as a <u>catharsis through which one emancipates</u> oneself.

Irony has a double function in this process: it exists as an interplay between narrator and character, as a dialectical consciousness immanent in the text; and irony, here, is also an aesthetic irony, i.e., an irony whose aim is to discard the literary material itself, to reject the literary content and form as being unsuitable for the attainment of meaning. This latter form of irony implies, then, that the narrator has been using an obsolete medium, that of the novel, to attain meaning; this type of irony also implies that the private language of the subjective universe provides the author with an incomplete insight into the world. Meaning has to be created, somehow, outside the fictional space. This indicates that there is a dialectic in Modernism, a dialectic which is often implied or concealed, but which is a manifestation of the negating influence of the consciousness of the text. It is very important to emphasize the presence of irony in the modern novel; in the absence of any political affiliation on part of the protagonists and authors, irony becomes the vehicle for a rebellion against the conditions of the modern world, and irony, therefore, can be interpreted as the method by which consciousness evolves inside the fictional space of the novel as well as outside of it. Contrary to Lukacs, then, I believe one can find change and development in the modern novel, although extreme cases such as *Ulysses* present a static universe and a static consciousness which fail to produce actual change; change only occurs on the levels of dream and wish fulfillment. But even *Ulysses* creates at least the illusion of a social and historical milieu, by providing us with a detailed "map" of Dublin, the home of Stephen Dedalus, Leopold

Bloom, and Molly Bloom. The use of the word "illusion" evokes Lukacs' expression "abstract particularity", which refers to the induction of an extreme accuracy of physical detail as a medium for a dreamlike vividness, a vividness which we find so abundantly in the works of Franz Kafka. The dreamlike, nightmarish quality of the world of <u>Ulysses</u> and of <u>The Trial</u> by Kafka is evoked precisely by this use of particular detail as a means of portraying <u>unreality</u>; the details are isolated phenomena, not part of a social, organic totality. Because of this inorganic use of detail, the protagonist of <u>The Trial</u> is at a loss when facing the "judges" and their habitation. Everything is unreal, abstract; Joseph K's relationship, his connection with external reality, has been severed. His case and his "guilt", therefore, appear unreal, and he is unable to understand the nature of it. The reason for there being a "case" at all is a result of his own lack of autonomy, his dissociation with reality. He must petition his case at "court", leaving it to others to decide it for him. His actions are non-actions, and he does not influence the course of events in the least. There are not any real "events", actually, since there are no real characters to instigate events; thus, the nature of Joseph K's guilt is never revealed to him - it is merely presented as being there, and the hero's attitude to it is passive. Kafka describes a very concrete circumstance in modern life, namely the impenetrability, or apparent impenetrability of the world around us, and his use of the bureaucratic class as representative of this imprenetrability is, of course, not accidental.

Even the modernist, "anti-realist" novel, however, leaves the protagonist and the reader some clues with which to decipher the world of the novel; the relationship between reader and novel may seem quite similar to that of the individual and the bureaucratic state in Kafka's novel. The reader must interpret the real relationships, relationships that are merely hinted at or perhaps even deliberately obscured behind the surface of abstract particularity. Demystifying the abstract, revealing the concrete behind it, can be seen as a political process involving the cognition of social and interpersonal relationships which do exist in reality, but which are made obscure through the process of communication itself. An obscure literary form expresses and represents an obscure social world. Distorted communication between individual and state in the modern world is reflected accurately in Kafka's novels; obscurity emulates and represents the individual's circumstances in real life. However, the narrator's consciousness distances itself from mere presentation through the use of irony and self-reflexiveness, as I pointed out earlier. The textual consciousness in this manner exposes a conflict between individual and world which can be overcome through an interpretation of the components of that conflict; through, that is, evolving a consciousness which <u>transcends the text itself while at the same time being immanent in it as its motivating impetus, as its reason for being</u>.

Although the reality examined in Modernism is static, the examining subject, the narrator, is in motion. Lukacs concedes that[3], but he does not perceive this as a dialectic promoting or expressing actual development, other than the gradual revelation of the human condition. The narrator moves above a static universe, and this stasis is part of an ontological absolute in Modernism, according to Lukacs. I differ with him here; I believe that Modernism transcends itself by revealing the static nature of reality, and the revelation becomes the first stage of a dynamic process which conducts us beyond the fictional space.

Lukacs' discussion of the ideology of Modernism, the ontology of solitariness, also focuses on the concept of potentiality, abstract and concrete. Abstract or subjective potentiality is an expression which refers to the innumerable possibilities in man's life, possibilities that are not realized unless one makes a choice to realize them, in which case they become concrete. In Modernism, imagined possibilities become synonymous with the actual complexities of life, and individuality loses its contours or boundaries; man is described as being in a state of flux, with limitless modes of existence open to him. The subject remains in a dream world unless he makes a choice to actualize his potentiality, chooses to become real. Abstract potentiality, then, belongs to the subjective realm of Modernism, or anti-realism, whereas concrete potentiality belongs to realism, where it functions as a dialectic between subjective and objective reality. Concrete potentiality identifies the characters of the novel and their space for us. If, however, reality is seen as a projection of abstract potentiality, then the characters will lose their identity. It is significant, for example, that the mythological figure Proteus plays such an important part in *Ulysses*. Proteus is the emblem of an abstract reality in constant flux, and the

Greek god symbolizes the intangible materialization of a mask or many masks, rather than actual identity. Everything can be exchanged for everything else; hence Stephen Dedulus' failure to capture and identify the fleeting nature of reality, the "ineluctable modality of the visible and the audible". The shape of Proteus becomes empty form, gesture without motion, and reality becomes impossible to pin down. The disintegration of identity and character in Modernism is thus "matched by a disintegration of the outer world".[4] The projection of the potential onto the actual produces an attenuation of reality, a voiding of reality. Consequently, subjective inwardness is exalted, and the protagonist's attempt to rationally explicate the world is aborted. Lukacs claims that this dissolution of personality is "the unconscious product of the identification of concrete and abstract potentiality";[5] or, the unconscious product of what I have called the projection of abstract potentiality onto actuality. I believe, however, that this process is not an unconscious one. The fact that Lukacs describes it as unconscious is, of course, consistent with his critique of Modernism, which is based upon his analysis of the ontology of solitariness. He believes that this ontology dominates the modernist tradition and that it is inserted as an implicit, obscure system of communication the presence of which is not clear, or conscious, to the author himself. However, it is my contention that signs, images, symbols, and characters are organized and presented consciously in the modern novel.

Lukacs traces the tradition of subjectiveness, inwardness, and the tradition of subjective idealism back to the mid-19th century, and he sees Søren Kierkegaard as one of the exponents of the ontology of solitariness. Kierkegaard did attack the Hegelian view that the internal and external world form an objective, dialectical unity. Kierkegaard denied this unity and claimed that the individual exists within an "incognito". But Kierkegaard's incognito is not an impenetrable one, as Lukacs believes. The incognito, according to Kierkegaard, is the manifest presence of the Infinite in the finite, God in the world. Man meets God in the world at a point in time called Øieblikket ;[6] and man becomes aware of God's presence only after having attained total subjectivity and concrete objective existence in the world. The process of cognition in Kierkegaard's stages, the aesthetical, ethical, and religious, form a religious hermeneutic, the goal of which is to strip away the illusions of the aesthete, thus making him choose individual, concrete existence in the ethical and religious stages. The individual chooses to take over his own self, to reveal himself to himself and others. Kierkegaard's function as a literary writer and as a religious writer is a pedagogical one, and Kierkegaard himself assumes an "incognito", a variety of pseudonyms which serve the purpose of seducing the reader into knowing himself. Kierkegaard concentrates, mainly, on seducing the aesthete (himself a seducer) into becoming ethical and religious, into concretizing his abstract potential. As a religious writer, Kierkegaard sees himself inhabiting a space in the world similar to that of God; he speaks to his audience "incognito", using the pseudonym in the dual function of hiding himself and revealing himself, in the same manner by which God is simultaneously hidden and revealed in Creation and in history. Kierkegaard's system can be described, therefore, as a hermeneutic which aims at restoring the individual to a meaningful existence *in the world*. Initially, the process of choosing oneself is a negation or renunciation of objectivity and a subsequent turning toward subjectivity. Truth is subjective because God is a subject; the aesthete must perform a negation of his life in the aesthetical mode, and this negation becomes a rejection of illusion. Kierkegaard exposes the multifarious, artistic experiments of the aesthete as being illusory attempts to create identity in a world which is not the real social, historical world. It is not real because the aesthete has not realized himself as <u>subject</u> in relation to it; he is not involved in it, but uses it as an object of artistic experiments. The life which the aesthete must renounce, prompted by the Kierkegaardian pseudonym Vilhelm in <u>Either-Or</u> (1843), is the life in abstract potentiality of which Lukacs speaks; Lukacs has thus misunderstood Kierkegaard's doctrine of the eternal incognito; it is not an empty transcendence, transcendence of Nothingness, or a higher potency of subjective, abstract potentiality; it is actual transcendence, promotion of concrete subjectivity in real history, through the induction of the individual into the ethical and religious stages. In these stages, life is not mere art, as in the aesthetical modality; it is realized concretely. Kierkegaard's dialectic, which is a dialectic of the subject's relation to itself, congrues in part with Marxian dialectics, because Kierkegaard exposes the world of commodities and self-alienation, the bourgeois world in which the aesthete lives; through negating this world Kierkegaard exposes the obscurity inherent in it, and he indicates how the aesthete obscures himself. Kierkegaard's philosophy, then, aims at deciphering and explicating the obscure and at recognizing truth. Self-realization is, of course, metaphysical as well as historical for Kierkegaard. The individual finds God when he finds himself in history. The trend of Kierkegaard's thought, the movement of the subject in relation to itself and to the object, could be seen as the progressive isolation and inward-turning of the individual, as the endowment of the subjective with a higher potency, if we were to use a Marxist analysis. But inwardness is only a stage in which the individual finds himself and his real place in history. Kierkegaard's philosophy is, rather, a progressive unfolding or revealing of the mid-19th century bourgeois world as illusion-ridden and <u>angst</u>-ridden. Kierkegaard's ethical demand, and his claim of the subjective Ideal, is a logical consequence of his rejection of philistine idealism. The claim of the ideal can be seen as potentially revolutionary, and Kierkegaard does not aim at creating an "abstract potentiality"; rather, he wants to create a concrete individuality, concrete existence in history. The proposition that Kierkegaard's philosophy and theology belongs to the realm of historicity is difficult to defend, but it depends, of course, on one's critical, ideological bias. It cannot be denied that Kierkegaard's exposure of the philistine world is quite as astute as that of Marx, and that Kierkegaard's awareness of the polarity of illusion and reality, although not the product of dialectical materialism, is based on a dialectic which negates illusion and affirms truth.

Frederic Jameson's definition of dialectical thought is useful in this connection:[7]

> ... dialectic thought is in its very structure self-consciousness and may be described as the attempt to think about a given object on one level, and at the same time to observe our own thought processes as we do so: or to use a more scientific figure, to reckon the position of the observer into the experiment itself. In this light, the difference between the Hegelian and the Marxist dialectics can be defined in terms of the type of self-consciousness involved. For Hegel this is a relatively logical one, and involves a sense of the interrelationship of such purely intellectual categories as subject and object, quality and quantity, limitation and infinity, and so forth; here the thinker comes to understand the way in which his own determinate thought processes, and indeed the very forms of the problems from which he sets forth, limit the results of his thinking. For the Marxist dialectic, on the other hand, the self-consciousness aimed at is the awareness of the thinker's position in society and in history itself, and of the limits imposed on this awareness by his class position - in short of the ideological and situational nature of all thought and of the initial invention of the problems themselves. Thus, it is clear that these two forms of the dialectic in no way contradict each other, even though their precise relationship remains to be worked out.

Jameson correctly points out that self-consciousness does not mean introspection; it should be seen as a process through which material elevates itself to awareness. There is congruence between the object of thought and the "set of mental operations proposed by the intrinsic nature of that particular object".[8] I see no disparity between this definition of dialectical thought and Kierkegaard's structural composition of the stages or modes of life in Either-Or and Stages on Life's Way (1845). Kierkegaard's pedagogical unfolding of self-consciousness is designed to induce a state of mind whereby material lifts itself to awareness. The structure of the stages is tripartite; the aesthete lives in the category of immediacy. He is controlled by outside stimuli and is thus subject to Fate. He has no commitment to the world, but uses it for his own exploitative ends - this is true, for example, of his relationship to women. The aesthete lives outside himself, and his being is multifarious, i.e., he is in a state of flux, without identity or continuity; he lives in that sphere of abstract potentiality of which Lukacs speaks; he remodels his life into a work of art. He obscures himself to himself and to others; this technique of self-concealment is consciously applied by the aesthete in order to control and manipulate others. His consciousness, however, is directed away from himself, not into himself; he is basically unconscious of his own self and has not yet chosen to be himself. The ethical person, by contrast, has assumed responsibility for himself, and has turned inward to know himself; that which is known to him also becomes exposed to others. The obscure or hidden, the previously unconscious, is revealed. The ethical modality is a negation of the aesthetical modality; the religious modality becomes a synthesis of the aesthetical and ethical in that it is both inwardly and outwardly oriented. The aesthete, however, was only naively related to relative ends, whereas the religious individual is seriously related to absolute ends.

The religious stage recaptures the aesthetical modality in its direction towards the external; but the external, social world is now a concrete world, not the world of philistine illusions; the religious individual has now chosen himself in actuality, through inwardness and inner awareness. The passion, or pathos, of the religious individual has become real, not just aesthetic. Unconscious material is thus elevated to self-consciousness and consciousness of other, a concrete other, not an abstract other. Kierkegaard's philosophy states in its own way that the object of thought is lifted to self-awareness through a particular set of mental operations. Kierkegaard's main criticism is, of course, directed towards the aesthete who has no concrete existence because he is as yet unconscious in relation to himself, and only conscious in relation to others. Kierkegaard's ultimate purpose was to make the aesthete come to awareness of the Infinite in the finite, to proceed from abstract to concrete existence. It is a mistake to define Kierkegaard's philosophy as subjective idealism, and we cannot place him within the tradition depicted by Lukacs as the ontology of solitariness. But Kierkegaard's development of the stages of life is important to our analysis of Modernism because the first stage, the aesthetical modality, can serve, in part, as a model for or structural parallel to the presentation of character in the modernist novel, and for the medium in which these characters live, the medium of obscurity and discontinuity.

A number of protagonists and authors in Modernism are the victims of a disrupted process of socialization, a disruption which often creates confused identity and lack of continuity, a feeling of unreality which parallels that of the aesthete. The aesthete's answer to his problem is to make life into a work of art, thus creating an aesthetic structure in the abstract; aesthetic form is a way of ordering existence and finding or expressing meaning, and "form" could be seen as the preliminary groping of the aesthete towards creating identity, a first, necessary stage in his development.

Knut Hamsun and other modernist writers use form in the same way. However, the use of form as an autonomous vehicle of meaning in Modernism contains its own contradiction, namely, the negation of form, the apparently total dissolution of form. We are faced with an ambivalence here, which in the case of Hamsun led to a confused identity and precipitation into Nazism. The author was split off from objective reality, a reality which he revealed in his writings, through his protagonists, but which he misinterpreted in his private life. Hamsun, the writer, was aware of the dangers of isolation but fell prey to those same dangers as a private person. Hamsun was propelled into that state of mind which Lukacs correctly refers to as unreality; infinite possibilities or potentialities became substituted for reality itself with the result that everything is exchangeable for everything else. Values are equalized and quantified, there are no concrete or absolute values. The dissolution of personality that took place in the novel <u>Hunger</u> became, interestingly enough, a parallel to Hamsun's own dissolution, causing him to search for meaning and identity within the wrong political party. This is an ironic comment on the substitution of art for life.

Lukacs would attribute this substitution of art for life to the ahistoricity of Modernism; the modernist writer does not, according to Lukacs, exhibit awareness of his position in society and history itself. Ahistoricity causes a lack of perspective, a departure from the genre of realism, where the hero developed identity and personality through interaction with the environment. Lukacs advocates a revival of the epic as a counterpart to Modernism, and Walter Benjamin speaks of the importance of storytelling as a literary form whose ideology promotes the idea of an autonomously acting hero, in his essay, "The Storyteller and Artisan Cultures" (1936).[9]

For Lukacs, the deprivation of a sense of perspective is related to the preoccupation, in Naturalism and Modernism, with psychopathology. Lukacs sees the tradition of introspection as inchoate in the Naturalist movement, and he views Sigmund Freud's psychopathology as emblematic of the tendency towards inwardness in modernist literature. Rather than dividing literary history into separate trends and movements, Lukacs' Marxist critique focuses on social-historical definitions of the modernist ontology, and he sees this ontology as part of an intellectual history extending from Naturalism. Lukacs contends that literature is part of a historical totality, a societal form, namely the socioeconomic organization that we call Capitalism. Both Naturalism and Modernism can, of course, be seen as forms of protest against Capitalism as a system which deprives the individual of his capacity for autonomous action. Psychopathology becomes a way of obviating boredom under Capitalism by looking for the abnormal. The presentation of character becomes more interesting that way, and the search for the abnormal is prevalent in Freud's writings, for example. Freud examined the abnormal mind in order to gain insight into the normal mind. Although the description of the abnormal is a form of protest, then, the Marxist critic points out that any protest against social conditions should emphasize the description of these conditions themselves instead of focusing on the isolated individual and the workings of the subconscious mind. Criticism of the old social order is a point of departure for the establishment of a new order, and Lukacs sees such criticism as being obscured by the Modernist attempt to present the individual in isolation. Modernism, in other words, is not constructive enough. By contrast, realism develops new types and genres for each phase of societal evolution, thus displaying the contradictions within society and within the individual in "the context of a dialectical unity",[10] as in the bourgeois revolt against Feudalism and the proletarian revolt against bourgeois society.[11]

Lukacs sees the polarity of the normal and the abnormal as an abstract typology, divorced from its social context. In order for literary typology to be concrete, the socially typical must be embodied in the particular or individual, and if a description of objective reality is lacking, that reality is reduced to dream or nightmare, as in Kafka's The Trial. The same is true of the vision of reality in the works of James Joyce, William Faulkner and Samuel Beckett, where we find perversion and idiocy exalted and glorified; Lukacs states that literature must have a concept of the normal if it is to evaluate eccentricity and distortion realistically, within a perspective. In Ulysses, however, we do find the normal, the average, represented in the character of Leopold Bloom, and normalcy and typicality are present in most, if not all, the novels I shall examine, and I intend to attempt a definition of the concretely typical in Modernism as I analyze the novels. In spite of this, however, I do agree with Lukacs, that social realism is the literary form most necessary to the expression of social relations; but this does not mean that social relations are not implied in Modernism, which I intend to show. "Inwardness" and "the subjective" in Modernism are part of a methodology through which the narrator or implied author writes himself through a stage of life, thus achieving catharsis. The cathartic effect of writing itself has ideological and philosophical implications; it indicates that the writer, as literary <u>agens</u>, searches actively for autonomy and identity instead of rejecting the idea of autonomy. Before autonomy can be achieved, and before a new dynamic can be evolved, a period of stasis and internal flux must be experienced and expressed in writing. This experience is often written down in retrospect, as in Hamsun's <u>Hunger</u> and Martin A. Hansen's <u>The Liar</u>, for example. For this reason, Naturalism and Modernism appear to be part of an identical ontology or ideology, the ideology of isolation and stasis. The dynamic element in literature, the evolution and formation of character, is suspended during the period of retrospective cognition; at the end of the novel <u>Hunger</u>, the protagonist sees the city from a new point of view as he leaves it. A new description, a new experience can begin. This fact contradicts Lukacs' assertion that the modernist sees outward reality as unalterable; the modernist, rather, creates a deliberate, a conscious suspension of social dynamics, which gives us the impression, perhaps, that the world, in Modernism, is what it is, that it cannot be different. However, as in Kierkegaard's philosophy, the subjective must be explored before the objective can be recognized concretely; the emotions which permeate inward reality are despair and anxiety <u>(angst)</u>; these emotions propel Kierkegaard's individual from one mode of life to another, from the aesthetic mode or the ethical mode to the religious modality. All three modes of life contain anxiety and despair, and the process which the Kierkegaardian subject goes through is not intellectually or logically motivated alone; it is motivated, moved along, by anxiety, by the perception and feeling of being alienated from oneself. Kierkegaard's analysis of despair made him depart radically from Hegel's logical system. From Kierkegaard's point of view, Hegel's logical formulations contradicted concrete reality, and

Kierkegaard's philosophy describes the transition from one existential mode to another as unmediated, abrupt, even traumatic. The individual achieves concrete existence through the emotional awareness of the conflicting poles of life, the finite and the Infinite, and these poles are concretely opposed to one another, not mediated. The awareness of conflict causes despair; despair and suffering become most outspoken, perhaps, in the ethical and religious stages, because the individual, here, chooses himself absolutely and concretely, whereas the self is only a potential, abstract self in the aesthetic stage. The aesthete remains fundamentally unchanged, although his life is multifarious, and he attempts to change the world only in an abstract sense. He is not involved in it; the pathos of the aesthete is aesthetic, artistically contrived, and he uses language as an artful game by which he maintains everything at the level of possibility, a level at which things cannot hurt him. The descent into inwardness in the ethical stage is necessary if the individual wants to become involved with himself and the world in seriousness. The ethical individual turns art into life.

Both trends are discernible in Modernism. The introverted subject in the modernist novel exhibits pathos, suffering and despair. The "writing through" this despair is a mechanism by which the writer endures the experience and achieves distance through irony and comedy. The dialectic of art and life, of subject and object, manifests itself in the aesthetic form as a controlling mechanism by which the modernist manipulates his material, much like Kierkegaard's aesthete. Distance, in the modernist novel, operates as an ironic perspective calculated to achieve at least the semblance of order and meaning, an order superimposed upon the apparently chaotic experience of the protagonist. Irony is also the method by which the chaotic material, immersed into unconsciousness, is elevated to consciousness. Consciousness of self becomes a pre-requisite for concrete existence in history.

In some of the novels I shall examine, this consciousness is negative; Pär Lagerkvist's novel The Dwarf, for example, presents a culturally pessimistic perspective through the reductive point of view of a cynical mind; in William Faulkner's novel As I Lay Dying, one of the characters, Darl, attempts to recognize objective reality, but is split off from himself, divided, and sent to an insane asylum; and Joyce's Ulysses remains a static universe from beginning to end, a dreaming, retrospective medium. Other novels present positive conclusions, as

Hamsun's <u>Hunger</u>, at the end of which the protagonist-narrator has lived through, written himself through experience and arrived at a new perception of his surroundings; the city, where he was imprisoned emotionally and intellectually, becomes a city of thousand lights. James Joyce's <u>A</u> <u>Portrait</u> <u>of</u> <u>the</u> <u>Artist</u> <u>as</u> <u>a</u> <u>Young</u> <u>Man</u> ends on a note of positive hope as the protagonist escapes from the imprisonment of Irish society. Yet other novels present ambivalent, open-ended solutions, e.g., Tom Kristensen's <u>Havoc</u>, which operates with an extra-fictional framework that at least hints at new directions for the protagonist; and Martin A. Hansen's <u>The</u> <u>Liar</u> evolves from literary production into a scientific, historical record, a development, however, which partly depends upon instinctual renunciation. Consciousness, in all of these novels, always exposes, reveals, and works its way through stagnating, static material in order to resolve past and present fixations. The literary process is not an extension of an unconscious ontology or ideology, but a result of a reaction to and rejection of that ontology. The ontology of solitariness, man's isolated condition, is transcended, in some of these novels, through self-consciousness. It is on the whole questionable whether we can speak of the unconscious as being ideological; ideology can, of course, be unconscious (the latter statement is the opposite of the former), but the modernist makes an attempt to elevate ideology into the light of consciousness; reason counteracts illusion, here.

The other side of Modernism is a de-valuation or depreciation of literary art itself, an art which perhaps does not adequately absorb the social conditions which determine its own existence, as Lukacs points out. The modernist does struggle with an empty transcendence, the higher potency of the subjective, which has no objective counterpart; but the higher potency of the subjective is also identical with the creative imagination, a fact that Lukacs does not take into account. It is Lukacs' intention to prove that Modernism substitutes the disintegration of man's world for the disintegration of society, that the modernist, in other words, turns a social problem into a metaphysical one. It is true that Modernism treats concrete social problems only indirectly, leaving the reader to decipher the relationship between the individual character and his environment. In realistic literature, detail is both individual and typical; but Lukacs claims that the typical is neglected in Modernism,[12] as mentioned above. I have attempted to indicate

how the mind of the protagonist works its way through
personal riddles and conflicts to a level of awareness
coinciding with that of the narrator, the level of
ironic anticipatory consciousness, a typical consciousness. Freud's analysis of the abnormal mind was only
a preliminary step towards the deciphering of obscurity,
not a preoccupation with the pathological as an end in
itself. His objective was, after all, to restore the
individual to normalcy through psychoanalysis. Paul
Ricoeur emphasizes this in his essay entitled "Hermeneutics: Restoration of Meaning or Reduction of Illusion?" (1965):

> What Freud desires is that the one who is
> analysed, by making his own the meaning that
> was foreign to him, enlarge his field of
> consciousness, live better, and finally be a
> little freer and, if possible, a little happier.
> One of the earliest homages paid to psycho-
> analysis speaks of 'healing through conscious-
> ness'. The phrase is exact - if one means
> thereby that analysis wishes to substitute
> for an immediate and dissimulating conscious-
> ness a mediate consciousness taught by the
> reality principle. Thus the same doubter
> who depicts the ego as a 'poor creature' in
> subjection to three masters, the id, the super-
> ego, and reality or necessity, is also the
> exegete who rediscovers the logic of the illog-
> ical kingdom and who dares, with unparalleled
> modesty and discretion, to terminate his essay
> on *The Future of an Illusion* by invoking the
> god Logos, soft of voice but indefatigable, in
> no wise omnipotent, but efficacious in the long
> run.[13]

Both Freud and Marx begin with a suspicion concerning the illusions of consciousness; Marx' term for this illusion of consciousness is "false consciousness", unawareness of one's own social situation; for Freud, illusion is a falsification of meaning, a distortion engaged upon by the neurotic patient. All three, Freud, Marx, and Kierkegaard, try to demystify illusion and create meaning through the revelation of truth, psychologically, socially, and theologically. The so-called discipline of reality or necessity advocated by Marx and Freud is paralleled in Lukacs' critical thinking when he discards Modernist ontology;[14] the infinitely possible, subjective potentiality, however, finds its concretion in Kierkegaard's philosophy; here it takes the form of the individual's absolute relationship with God; the individual meets God in history.

Hermeneutics, as an art of interpreting, has the dual function of destroying and constructing; I find both of these principles to be inherent in Modernism as well as in Kierkegaard's philosophy. The subjective potential, which Lukacs speaks of, is not only illusion, but part of the concrete activity of the creative imagination, which reveals and restores meaning through the word, *Logos*. In the words of Paul Ricoeur, "the 'conscious' methods of deciphering coincide with the unconscious work of 'ciphering'",[15] in other words, that which I have called the narrator "writing himself through" an experience, thus transcending it. We do not, of course, find traces of Kierkegaard's theology, his belief in God, in Modernism. God is absent in the modernist novel, and meaning is here related to a gradual revelation of individual repression and societal oppression; such revelation is emancipatory in the sense that the modern subject, much like Freud's neurotic patient, is opened up to himself and to others through writing about himself. This subject to subject dialogue, the self-reflexiveness of Modernism, involves introspection, dissolution, and analysis. But the analysis is a conscious, rational one; inherent in this rationality is still the belief that man is able to penetrate the secrets of the world; although Freud chose the area of abnormality for his clinical study, his method was still scientific, rational, and involved the deciphering of neurotic illusions and fixations.

Marxist criticism views Modernism, in short, as a literary tradition that describes the individual as divorced from his social context; the human subject, in modernist art, projects its own internal reality onto external reality; this process produces the objectification of the subject; objectification, here, is not identical to the recreation of a subject-object dialectic. Rather, it is the projection of the lyrical, imaginative self, which searches for meaning, into an empty transcendence, or empty ideality, an ideality which has no concrete, or real, existence. The lyrical subject in the modernist mode seeks to attain happiness, but finds it to be unattainable, non-existent, and therefore reacts by destroying and rejecting reality itself, by describing reality with signs, images and symbols which express dissolution and chaos. This is what Lukacs refers to as the dissolution of reality in Modernism, and the dual motion of seeking identity and destroying reality could be called the dialectics of Modernism. Empirical reality is seen as being insufficient for the transcendental pathos of the modern subject; this entails not only a dichotomy, a dissonance, between the human subject and objective reality, but also a dissonance in the subject itself, a split between the lyrical, imaginary self and the empirical or actual social self. This split manifests itself as a de-personalization, by which the personal is turned into something suprapersonal; the subject is objectified. The creative subject, through self-examination, recognizes its own limitations, its own limited space and compensates for it by evoking a world which contains infinite potential. Marxist criticism interprets this process as a continuous reproduction of the same static material, as we indeed see in <u>Ulysses</u>, as abstract, ever-recurring variations on the same theme. The tension between "lyrical" and "empirical" self, between self and social world, and finally, between an abstract, imaginary space and concrete, threatening reality produces a negation and distortion of the actual social relationships. The creative imagination, in the Marxist interpretation, has turned into a dictatorial imagination, which imposes its imagery, symbols, and concepts on reality. The attenuation of actual reality produces a lack of political potential in modernistic art.

I have indicated that Modernism does have political potential, due to the emancipatory work of consciousness. Herbert Marcuse says that he sees the "political potential of art in art itself, in the aesthetic form as such."[16] Marcuse states that the movements of Expressionism and Surrealism anticipated the destructiveness of monopoly capitalism, rather than passively reflecting this destructiveness; and that, by virtue of the aesthetic form itself, any work of art is <u>revolutionary</u> in that it represents an indictment of established reality and creates the "appearance of the image of liberation".[17] Marcuse elucidates this statement as follows:

> . . . the radical qualities of art, that is to say, its indictment of the established reality and its invocation of the beautiful image (*schöner Schein*) of liberation are grounded precisely in the dimensions where art *transcends* its social determination and emancipates itself from the given universe of discourse and behavior while preserving its overwhelming presence. Thereby art creates the realm in which the subversion of experience proper to art becomes possible: the world formed by art is recognized as a reality which is suppressed and distorted in the given reality. This experience culminates in extreme situations (of love and death, guilt and failure, but also joy, happiness, and fulfillment) which explode the given reality in the name of a truth normally denied or even unheard. The inner logic of the work of art terminates in the emergence of another reason, another sensibility, which defy the rationality and sensibility incorporated in the dominant social institutions.
> Under the law of the aesthetic form, the given reality is necessarily *sublimated*: the immediate content is stylized, the "data" are reshaped and reordered in accordance with the demands of the art form, which requires that even the representation of death and destruction invoke the need for hope — a need rooted in the new consciousness embodied in the work of art.[18]

The emancipation of art from the "given universe of discourse and behavior" creates a second reality, that reality which is "suppressed and distorted in the given reality". This is not false consciousness, or the illusory objectification of the subject, but a counter-consciousness, an emancipatory consciousness. Aesthetic form is a social-historical phenomenon, but it also transcends the social and the historical.

The novels which I shall discuss in this book are concerned primarily with the creation of aesthetic form; they are about the creative process itself; the protagonists are themselves writers or artists, struggling with their own birth process. In these novels, revolution is not thematic, but can be seen to be implied in the literary form, through the creation of a second reality.

Before examining the literary works themselves, I shall analyze Søren Kierkegaard's existential modalities and two works by Sigmund Freud in order to further elucidate the emancipatory consciousness inherent in the work of art.

INTRODUCTION REFERENCES

[1] Georg Lukacs, *The Meaning of Contemporary Realism* (London: Merlin Press, 1962) p. 19.

[2] Lukacs, p. 20.

[3] Lukacs, p. 21.

[4] Lukacs, p. 25.

[5] Lukacs, p. 26.

[6] The "moment" - in Kierkegaard's terminology, this is the point of intersection between the finite and the Infinite.

[7] Frederic Jameson, *Marxism and Form* (Princeton, New Jersey: Princeton University Press, 1971) p. 340.

[8] Jameson, p. 341.

[9] Walter Benjamin, "The Story Teller and Artisan Cultures," in *Critical Sociology*, ed. Paul Connerton (London: Hazell Watson & Viney Ltd, Aylesbury, Bucks, 1976) p. 277.

[10] Lukacs, p. 31.

[11] In the literature of the late sixties and the seventies in Denmark, there was a revival of the genre

of social realism in the so-called Arbejderroman
(Worker's Novel).

¹²Lukacs, p. 43.

¹³Paul Ricoeur, "Hermeneutics: Restoration of
Meaning or Reduction of Illusion?" in Critical Sociology,
ed. Paul Connerton (London: Hazell Watson & Viney Ltd,
Aylesbury, Bucks, 1976) p. 202.

¹⁴I shall discuss this in detail in my analysis of
Freud's Beyond the Pleasure Principle and Civilization
and Its Discontents.

¹⁵Ricoeur, in Critical Sociology, p. 201.

¹⁶Herbert Marcuse, The Aesthetic Dimension - Toward
a Critique of Marxist Aesthetics (Boston: Beacon Press,
1978) p. IX.

¹⁷Marcuse, p. XI.

¹⁸Marcuse, pp. 6-7.

CHAPTER 1

FREEDOM AND COMMUNICATION ACCORDING TO KIERKEGAARD

A. <u>The Concept ov Anxiety</u>

Søren Kierkegaard developed his concept of <u>angst</u>, anxiety or dread, in <u>The Concept of</u> Anxiety (1844), which was authored by one of the pseudonyms, Vigilius Haufniensis (the "vigilant Copenhagener"). The concept of anxiety functions as an important part of Vigilius' anthropological theory, which encompasses two different but intimately connected dialectical theses: body-soul-spirit, and the temporal-the eternal-the moment. Vigilius analyzes the first dialectical process as follows:

> That anxiety makes its appearance is the pivot upon which everything turns. Man is a synthesis of the psychical and the physical; however, a synthesis is unthinkable if the two are not united in a third. This third is spirit. In innocence, man is not merely animal, for if he were at any moment of his life merely animal, he would never become man. So spirit is present, but as immediate, as dreaming. Inasmuch as it is now present, it is in a sense a hostile power, for it constantly disturbs the relation between soul and body, a relation that indeed has persistence and yet does not have endurance, inasmuch as it first receives the latter by the spirit. On the other hand, spirit is a friendly power, since it is precisely that which constitutes the relation. What, then, is man's relation to this ambiguous power? How does spirit relate itself to itself and to its conditionality? It relates itself as anxiety.

> Do away with itself, the spirit cannot; lay hold of itself, it cannot, as long as it has itself outside of itself. Nor can man sink down into the vegetative, for he is qualified as spirit; flee away from anxiety, he cannot, for he loves it; really love it, he cannot, for he flees from it. Innocence has now reached its uttermost point. It is ignorance; however, it is not an animal brutality but an ignorance qualified by spirit, and as such innocence is precisely anxiety, because its ignorance is about nothing. Here there is no knowledge of good and evil etc., but the whole actuality of knowledge projects itself in anxiety as the enormous nothing of ignorance.[1]

Man, in his innocent, pre-conscious state, is made up of body, soul, and spirit, but the spirit is present in a dreaming state only; it is not yet fully unfolded or conscious. <u>Angst</u> is an emotional state expressing fear of becoming conscious; <u>angst</u> is also the fear of remaining unconscious. In the unconscious state, spirit is only potentially or latently present, and its absence produces the fear of nothingness, which is anxiety. Vigilius also interprets the state of unconsciousness as a state of not being free, and anxiety becomes a fear of becoming free, a fear of the possibility of freedom. At a later point in his analysis, Vigilius connects the first dialectical movement with a second one:

> Man, then, is a synthesis of psyche and body, but he is also a <u>synthesis</u> <u>of</u> <u>the</u> <u>temporal</u> <u>and</u> <u>the</u> <u>eternal</u>. That this often has been stated, I do not object to at all, for it is not my wish to discover something new, but rather it is my joy and dearest occupation

> to ponder over that which is quite simple.
> As for the latter synthesis, it is immediately striking that it is formed differently from the former. In the former, the two factors are psyche and body, and spirit is the third, yet in such a way that one can speak of a synthesis only when spirit is posited. The latter synthesis has only two factors, the temporal and the eternal. Where is the third factor? And if there is no third factor, there really is no synthesis, for a synthesis that is a contradiction cannot be completed as a synthesis without a third factor, because the fact that the synthesis is a contradiction asserts that it is not. What, then, is the temporal? 2

After having explained how man is a synthesis of the temporal and the eternal, Vigilius asks the question, what the third part of this second synthesis could be; his answer is that it is the moment, Øjeblikket. He defines "the moment" as follows:

> The moment is that ambiguity in which time and eternity touch each other, and with this the concept of temporality is posited, whereby time constantly intersects eternity and eternity constantly pervades time. As a result, the above-mentioned division acquires its significance: the present time, the past time, the future time.
> By this division, attention is immediately drawn to the fact that the future in a certain sense signifies more than the present and the past, because in a certain sense the future is the whole of which the past is a part, and the future can in a certain sense signify the whole. This is because the eternal first signifies the future or because the future is the incognito in which the eternal, even though it is incommensurable with time, nevertheless preserves its association with time. 3

The synthesis of the temporal and the eternal, in other words, is not separate from the synthesis of body and soul, but a manifestation of it. Spirit is created with the arrival of the moment. The moment, then, is the point of intersection between time and eternity. Spirit, as consciousness of the moment, is consciousness of the eternal and the temporal, i.e., history. Through man's coming to consciousness of the moment, he becomes conscious of his place as an individual in history. "Angst" is the psychological manifestation of the latency of spirit and moment in man. <u>Angst</u> is also the emotional prerequisite for the arrival of "spirit" and "moment". Vigilius defines this arrival as <u>freedom</u>. The possibility of becoming free causes anxiety, or rather, it is identified with anxiety.

> Thus the moment is there for Adam as well as for every subsequent individual. The synthesis of the psychical and the physical is to be posited by spirit; but spirit is eternal, and the synthesis is, therefore, only when spirit posits the first synthesis along with the second synthesis of the temporal and the eternal. As long as the eternal is not introduced, the moment is not, or is only a <u>discrimen</u> (boundary). Because in innocence spirit is qualified only as dreaming spirit, the eternal appears as the future, for this is, as has been said, the first expression of the eternal, and its incognito. Just as (in the previous chapter) the spirit, when it is about to be posited in the synthesis, or,

> more correctly, when it is about to posit the
> synthesis as the spirit's (freedom's) possibility
> in the individuality, expresses itself as anxiety,
> so here the future in turn is the eternal's (freedom's)
> possibility in the individuality expressed as anxiety.[4]

Vigilius' anthropology, as it is expressed in the bipartite dialectical movement above, conceives of the individual human being as dualistic. The individual manifests and creates the dualism of body and soul, which are the dual qualities or properties of spirit. Body, or nature, is the "outwardness", or outward expression of spirit; soul is the "inwardness", or internal manifestation of spirit. Spirit exists in the universal and in the particular. Translated to anthropological terms, the universal is the species, the particular the individual human subject. The individual body is the particular, the individual soul is the universal, or the general. Spirit is present in nature as dreaming spirit only; it is immersed in nature. But spirit also achieves a higher level of manifestation, namely in the individual consciousness. In nature, spirit was dreaming; it was outside itself. In the individual human subject, spirit comes to itself, awakens; it is made conscious and therefore free. The individual subject's body and soul are separate, but at the same time inseparate, correlated, the soul being the immanent objective of the body, that which the body is destined to become. The body functions, namely, as a system of organs, an organism; the soul is the creative union of these organs, the unifying principle of the physical organism. Since the body and soul are separate, but yet inseparate parts of the same unity or dual manifestations of the same purpose in nature, it follows that the human individual not only manifests a dualism, but also negates that same dualism. This negation is expressed, in the individual, as body and soul permeating each other; every bodily sensation and feeling is <u>spiritualized</u>, and every spiritual state is given bodily expression. The further this process progresses, the further is the body-soul dualism negated or reduced.

As we have seen, spirit is both part of the species and of the individual, the universal and the particular; spirit coming-to-itself means that spirit is manifested in the individual as a synthesis of the universal, soul, and the particular, body. Soul is the primary manifestation of spirit, body the primary manifestation of soul. By synthesizing the body-soul antithesis, the human individual becomes a unity of the general and the particular, i.e., the individual becomes what he is, a concrete subject. The creation of real subjectivity is a consequence of the spirit realizing itself as <u>individual</u> <u>self-consciousness</u>.

For Vigilius, the transition from dreaming spirit to spirit, or self-consciousness, is a qualitative leap whereby spirit negates nature and becomes free, and whereby the human subject frees itself and attains concrete existence.

> In innocence, Adam as spirit was a dreaming spirit. Thus the synthesis is not actual, for the combining factor is precisely the spirit, and as yet this is not posited as spirit. In animals the sexual difference can be developed instinctively, but this cannot be the case with a human being precisely because he is a synthesis. In the moment the spirit posits itself, it posits the synthesis, but in order to posit the synthesis it must first pervade it differentiatingly, and the ultimate point of the sensuous is precisely the sexual. Man can attain this ultimate point only in the moment the spirit becomes actual. Before that time he is not animal, but neither is he really man. The moment he becomes man, he becomes so by being animal as well.[5]

The evolution of spirit, in the individual, is precipitated by "<u>angst</u>" and by awakening sexuality. Sexuality is one of the concrete manifestations of self-consciousness through which creation approximates spirit, and through which dreaming spirit becomes real spirit. Attainment of real spirit, in religious terms, is reconciliation, the "moment" which synthesizes the body-soul antithesis. Vigilius defines sexuality as sensuality in the extreme; sensuality in the extreme is at the furthest opposite pole from spirituality. Sexuality, as an integral part of self-consciousness, approximated spirit and negated nature, or the instinctive, unconscious state; but since sexuality is "sensuality in the extreme", it also produced alienation, i.e., estrangement from the spirit, which Vigilius defines as original sin.[6]

Sexuality also creates, or re-creates, a new dualism in nature, because sexuality means awareness of sexual difference, the division of nature into male and female. The paradoxical meaning of sexuality and self-consciousness is, then, that they produce the awakening of the spirit, and at the same time, they posit the male-female dualism, a new loss of synthesis. It becomes the ethical obligation of the Christian individual to renounce the erotic life; this renunciation, according to Vigilius, will entail the closest possible approximation to spirit. Renunciation becomes part of an ethical ideal. According to Vigilius' formulations, one of the differences between men and women is that women have more angst because they are more sensual. The paradoxical meaning of sensuality has been defined, above, as the simultaneous approximation to and estrangement from spirit.

Sexual awareness contains <u>angst</u> as a premonition of the possible freedom of the self, the coming to consciousness. There is angst before consciousness, because the potentiality of freedom is anxiety-ridden; and there is angst after the arrival of consciousness because the reality of freedom is also anxiety-ridden. Vigilius formulates the relationship between anxiety and freedom:

> Anxiety may be compared with dizziness. He whose eye happens to look down into the yawning abyss becomes dizzy. But what is the reason for this? It is just as much in his own eye as in the abyss, for suppose he had not looked down. Hence anxiety is the dizziness of freedom, which emerges when the spirit wants to posit the synthesis and freedom looks down into its own possibility, laying hold of finiteness to support itself. Freedom succumbs in this dizziness. Further than this, psychology cannot and will not go. In that very moment everything is changed, and freedom, when it again rises, sees that it is guilty. Between these two moments lies the leap, which no science has explained and which no science can explain. He who becomes guilty in anxiety becomes as ambiguously guilty as it is possible to become. Anxiety is a feminine weakness in which freedom faints. Psychologically speaking, the fall into sin always takes place in weakness. But anxiety is of all things the most selfish, and no concrete expression of freedom is as selfish as the possibility of every concretion. This again is the overwhelming factor that determines the individual's ambiguous relation, sympathetic and antipathetic. In anxiety there is the selfish infinity of possibility, which does not tempt like a choice but ensnaringly disquiets (<u>aengster</u>) with its sweet anxiousness (<u>Beaengstelse</u>). 7

The possibility of becoming free creates an ambivalent anxiety: it is both sympathetic and antipathetic; it wants freedom and is afraid of it at the same time. <u>Angst</u> is the state of being afraid to remain unconscious, and it is the state of being afraid to become free, to become a concrete self; and angst is the object of more reflection in women than in men:

> The derivation of woman also contains an explanation of the sense in which she is weaker than man, something that in all times has been assumed, whether it is a pasha speaking or a romantic knight. Nevertheless, the difference is not such that man and woman are not essentially alike despite the dissimilarity. The expression for the difference is that anxiety is reflected more in Eve than in Adam. This is because woman is more sensuous than man. Obviously, the point here is not an empirical state or an average, but the dissimilarity in the synthesis. If in one part of the synthesis there is a "more", a consequence will be that when the spirit posits itself the cleft becomes deeper and that in freedom's possibility anxiety will find a greater scope. In the Genesis account, it is Eve who seduces Adam. But from this it in no way follows that her guilt is greater than Adam's, and still less that anxiety is an imperfection; on the contrary, the greatness of anxiety is a prophecy of the greatness of the perfection. 8

Despite the fact that women are more sensual than men, women are equally defined and determined by spirit. Men and women have equality of spirit; and sexuality must exist as a <u>sine qua non</u> for the historical evolution of the species, for which men and women are equally important.⁹

Men and women have an equal ethical obligation, also, to become free, to become autonomous, acting individuals, concrete subjects. Sexuality is the prerequisite for self-consciousness and for the achievement of selfhood; the negation of sexuality is the fulfillment of an ethical ideal, which is transformed into action in the ethical mode of life. Action is the realization of the good, and the pre-condition for this realization is the renunciation, not of the self, but of the <u>selfish</u>, that which is afraid to open up, to communicate, that which is enclosed within itself. Being enclosed within oneself is being demonic, in Vigilius' interpretation. The demonic is an inversion of the good and of truth; and <u>angst</u> reaches its highest level of manifestation in the demonic state of being, because the demonic is afraid of becoming itself openly and afraid of becoming free. The demonic is a conscious state of unfreedom, imprisonment; it is a maintained division from self, from spirit.

> The individual is in sin, and his anxiety is about the evil. Viewed from a higher standpoint, this formation is in the good, and for this reason it is in anxiety about the evil. The other formation is the demonic. The individual is in the evil and is in

> anxiety about the good. The bondage of sin is an
> unfree relation to the evil, but the demonic is an
> unfree relation to the good.
> The demonic therefore manifests itself clearly
> only when it is in contact with the good, which
> comes to its boundary from the outside. For this
> reason, it is noteworthy that the demonic in the New
> Testament first appears when it is approached by Christ.
> Whether the demon is legion (cf. Matthew 8:28-34; Mark
> 5:1-20; Luke 8:26-39) or is dumb (cf. Luke 11:14), the
> phenomenon is the same, namely, anxiety about the good,
> for anxiety can just as well express itself by muteness
> as by a scream. The good, of course, signifies the
> restoration of freedom, redemption, salvation, or
> whatever one would call it. 10

The demonic state entails a loss of freedom, and it produces silence, a state of not communicating with freedom, or with other, with that which is outside oneself. Paradoxically, not communicating with freedom is a form of communication, namely a betrayal or revelation of unfreedom, a revelation which can be verbal. The demonic mind communicates its own unfreedom against its will.

> The demonic is anxiety about the good. In innocence,
> freedom was not posited as freedom: its possibility
> was anxiety in the individual. In the demonic, the
> relation is reversed. Freedom is posited as unfreedom,
> because freedom is lost. Here again freedom's possi-
> bility is anxiety. The difference is absolute, because
> freedom's possibility appears here in relation to
> unfreedom, which is the very opposite of innocence,
> which is a qualification disposed toward freedom.
> The demonic is unfreedom that wants to close itself
> off. This, however, is and remains an impossibility.

> It always retains a relation, and even when this
> has apparently disappeared altogether, it is never-
> theless there, and anxiety at once manifests itself in
> the moment of contact (with the good) (see what is said
> above of the accounts in the New Testament).
> The demonic is <u>inclosing reserve</u> (det <u>Indesluttede</u>)
> and the <u>unfreely</u> <u>disclosed.</u> The two definitions indicate,
> as intended, the same thing, because inclosing reserve
> is precisely the mute, and when it is to express it-
> self, this must take place contrary to its will, since
> freedom, which underlies unfreedom or is its ground,
> by entering into communication with freedom from with-
> out, revolts and now betrays unfreedom in such a way
> that it is the individual who in anxiety betrays him-
> self against his will. 11

Unfreedom, which is a convoluted state of consciousness, a form of mind whose goal it is not to reveal or to become revealed, is the suppression of reality, a rejection of the potentiality of freedom and self-consciousness; the demonic mind also discards the ethical good. Vigilius defined "ethical good" as self-consciousness and as an attempt to approximate spirit through becoming that concrete subject which has synthesized body and soul, the temporal and the eternal. Achieving spirit means becoming real. Reality is the opposite of nothingness, and since Vigilius defines anxiety as the fear of nothingness, it follows that the demonic state of mind manifests the highest degree and quality of anxiety. The demonic does not enclose itself with "something", but is enclosed in its own nothingness, its own absence of reality.

The demonic mind deliberately, consciously rejects the good, which can only be achieved through communicating with self and through communicating self to other; in communicating self to other, one interacts with the world and acts in it. The demonic mind has lost freedom and reality; and this loss can be seen as the result of a division of the self, as consciousness divided from itself, and as a result of the division between self and other, subject and world. The demonic, then, communicates nothing but its own unfreedom; unfreedom has become imprisoned with itself.

> The demonic does not close itself up with something, but it closes itself up within itself, and in this lies what is profound about existence (<u>Tilvaerelsen</u>), precisely that unfreedom makes itself a prisoner. Freedom is always <u>communicerende</u> (communicating) (it does no harm even to take into consideration the religious significance of the word); unfreedom becomes more and more inclosed (<u>indesluttet</u>) and does not want communication. 12

The unwillingness to communicate produces a suppression of reality and a distortion of the language which denotes and symbolizes reality. The demonic personality has inverted its own relationship to the good and to truth and has become engaged in a monologue with itself, a monologue which expresses its own unfreedom. The language of unfreedom is characterized by a convoluted style, by circumlocutions of the truth; unfreedom exists in a state of anxiety which becomes an integral part of its own suppressed reality. The demonic mind communicates neither with self, nor with other, except by a distorted, obscure language that is designed to conceal the truth. The demonic is an inversion of truth contrived to prolong the state of imprisonment. Unfreedom becomes a static form of consciousness which does not conceive of the dialectical, but which still relates to something outside itself, in spite of itself; it relates inversely to freedom because freedom approaches it from the outside and wants to force it to come out, i.e., to commence the dialectical movement towards synthesis, towards spirit. The logical implication of this is that unfreedom can only be conceived of in relation to its own opposite, freedom. Unfreedom, logically and psychologically, is forced to communicate with freedom. The mind that is enclosed in itself is <u>det indesluttede</u>, a form of consciousness which only reveals itself in the manner I have described - by obscurity, and by hiding itself in a form which is not the form of the true self. The demonic mind creates an <u>incognito</u>. This incognito is the essence of aesthetic or poetic existence.

> It may will disclosure, but <u>incognito</u>. (This is the subtle contradiction of inclosing reserve, examples

> of which are found in poet-existences.) Disclosure
> may already have conquered; however, at the same
> moment, inclosing reserve ventures the last attempt
> and is ingenious enough to transform the disclosure
> itself into a mystification, and inclosing reserve
> has conquered. 13

Truth becomes mystified; the demonic has an awareness of what truth is, but hides from it in <u>angst</u>. The demonic is ambiguous, in that it fears its own nothingness as well as the revelation of reality. The function of the obscure language of the imprisoned mind is to deflect truth by lying; the selfishness of the demonic mind is thus a deflection from self.

B. The Seducer

Johannes Forføreren, the Seducer, appears in two of Kierkegaard's works, <u>Diary of a Seducer</u> (1843), which is part of <u>Either-Or</u>, and <u>Stages on Life's Way</u> (1845) where he addresses his friends on the topic of women and love in the section called "In Vino Veritas". Vigilius, the author of <u>The Concept of Anxiety</u>, analyzed the body-soul dualism as an aspect of the antithesis between the temporal and the eternal, which are synthesized in spirit; the synthesis was produced by consciousness which lifted the spirit out of its dreaming state; sexuality,

Vigilius argued, was an integral part of human self-consciousness. Sexuality re-posited a fundamental dualism, the sexual difference between man and woman. Vigilius interpreted sexuality, then, as ambivalent: it was part of the dialectical motion towards spirit, and at the same time it produced estrangement from spirit. Man and woman participate equally in the dialectical motion towards spirit.

According to Johannes the Seducer, however, sexual difference is absolute, not relative. Men are determined as spirit, women as sensuality. Johannes identifies women with "dreaming" spirit, and men with reflection and freedom; Johannes sees the unconscious dream state of the feminine psyche as the object of male reflection. Man's reflection brings woman out into a brief moment of sexual awareness and self-conscious freedom. Feminine nature is the external pole of male consciousness, its other self, or rather, the other part of itself. The brief moment of female freedom occurs as a qualitative leap; but woman loses her freedom almost immediately after having gained it. Her self-consciousness, which posited her as spirit and as sexual being, was created by the seducer, not by herself. Johannes says that she is "being for other", not being for self. She is interesting for others, not interesting to herself. Her moment of freedom is quickly lost and her identity is lost with it, hidden, so to speak, in the being of her seducer who contains and holds its secret. Since Johannes sees man as determined by spirit, and woman as not determined by spirit, a fundamental inequality is posited between the sexes; this inequality forms the basis of the Seducer's *modus operandi*, his method of seducing, the essence of which is to make women become attracted to their own opposite, namely (male) reflection; reflection is that part of them that they have not as yet realized. Women, in Johannes' conceptualization, thus become nature divided from spirit, and men become spirit divided from nature. The two assume a bi-polar relationship, a relationship of mutual dependency and dialectical interaction. The male-female dialectic does not, in Johannes' scheme of things, produce a synthesis; it only confirms and further consolidates the sexual polarity.

Vigilius and Johannes do concur on one thing, though: Women have more anxiety than men; anxiety, *angst*, is the dimly envisioned possibility of freedom, for women; *angst* becomes synonymous with love, because love unfolds the feminine being and creates it as spirit.

Diary of a Seducer belongs to the part of *Either-Or* which deals with the aesthetic mode of life. In her state of "dreaming spirit", woman is only aesthetically free; her freedom is in a naive, innocent stage, since she has not yet gone through the stage of doubt and reflection. Johannes' claim that woman is only briefly in a state of free consciousness is indicative of his own limitation. The fact that both man and woman are determined by spirit is an insight that Johannes rejects because he himself is divided between substance (the female) and reflection (the male), and this division produces his estrangement from spirit. Johannes has not progressed to the ethical and religious stages, but remains an aesthete whose life consists in manipulating women into a state of consciousness. His control of women is due to his reflective faculty which permeates the feminine being as that being's foreign element. Reflection is alien to women as nature is alien to Johannes; the two are divided from one another.

Johannes describes this division in mythical terms, in the banquet section of *Stages on Life's Way*; this section is entitled "In Vino Veritas", a title which accurately anticipates what takes place at the dinner table. "Truth in wine" is truth reflected, but distorted in a magical mirror. Johannes' topic is women, not as they are, but as he sees them; the feminine as a projection of the intoxicated masculine mind, whose limited perspective creates a semblance of truth, not truth itself. Johannes makes an account of how the Greek gods created man, but later divided him because they became jealous of his strength and wholeness. Woman was the product of the division. She was created to tempt man to his fall through her beauty. But, according to Johannes, a minority of men see through this beauty and turn it to their advantage by manipulating women into self-consciousness, which becomes their fall. Beauty, as interpreted by the Seducer, is the purely aesthetic semblance of spirit, dreaming spirit, not awakened spirit. By awakening women to their selves in angst and freedom, the Seducer controls them. Johannes adds:

> ... man is the one who was divided. At first, woman relates to man equally in the subdivision. She is a delusion, but not until the second moment, and only to the person who is deluded. She is the finite; but at first she is the finite intensified by the false infinity of all divine and human illusions. Deceit does not yet exist. But one moment later one is deceived. She is the finite and is thus a collectivum; one woman is many women. Only the lover understands this, and therefore he loves many women and is never deceived, but imbibes all the sensual

> pleasure that shrewd gods are capable of preparing
> for him. Therefore woman cannot be exactly defined,
> but is an infinity of finite possiblities. If a
> person wants to conceptualize the idea of woman, he
> will end up like someone staring into a sea of con-
> stantly changing nebulous images, or like someone who
> is bewildered by the aspect of foamy waves whose femi-
> nine shapes constantly delude, for the idea of woman
> is only a workshop of possibility, and for the lover,
> again, this possibility is the eternal source of
> erotic passion. (J.V.) 14

Spirit is only potentially present in women; women are finite and can, therefore, be multiplied infinitely, in the shapes of multiple bodies that are the materialized forms of the female soul. The Seducer, therefore, loves many women, not one. The one *is* the many. Johannes is a variation of Don Juan.

Johannes could have supplemented his deficient comprehension of the male-female relationship with another Greek myth, the myth of Pythia and her service at the Delphi oracle. Pythia, who is poised on a stool, receives intoxicating vapors from the earth beneath her and the words of the gods from above her. She is possessed, both by Phallos, or Eros, and Logos, by sexual being and reflective consciousness. The feminine being thus embodies a synthesis of sexuality and consciousness. Man, on the other hand, is divided in his meeting with the Sphinx; he perceives the Sphinx itself to be composed of fragments that he is unable to put together into a meaningful totality: human speech, wings of a bird, the body of a lion, the breasts of a woman. The Sphinx asks man the question, "What is it that has a voice, four legs, two legs, and three legs?" Man cannot give the answer, which is that this creature is a <u>human being</u>, composed of logos, voice or consciousness, and stick, phallos, or sexuality, and he is torn apart by the Sphinx. Man's motion towards woman, his progressive consciousness of her, leads through fragmentation; woman is totality, man division. This elucidates Johannes' limitations and his attitude that women are not determined by spirit; his interpretation is determined by the projection of his own divided consciousness onto other, woman. The Seducer, in accordance with his reductive view of femininity, describes her spirit as vegetating:

> This being of woman (for the word <u>existence</u> is too rich in meaning, since woman does not persist in and through herself) is rightly described as charm, an expression which suggests plant life; she is a flower, as the poets like to say, and even the spiritual in her is present in a vegetative manner. She is wholly subject to Nature, and hence only aesthetically free. In a deeper sense she first becomes free by her relation to man, and when man courts her properly, there can be no question of a choice. Woman chooses, it is true, but if this choice is thought of

> as the result of a long deliberation, then this choice is unfeminine. Hence it is, that it is a humiliation to receive a refusal, because the individual in question has rated himself too high, has desired to make another free without having the power. - In this situation there is deep irony. That which merely exists for another has the appearance of being predominant: man sues, woman chooses. The very concept of woman requires that she be vanquished; the concept of man, that he be the victor; and yet the victor bows before the vanquished. And yet this is quite natural, and it is only boorishness, stupidity, and lack of erotic sensibility to take no notice of that which immediately yields in this fashion. It has also a deeper ground. Woman is, namely, substance, man is reflection. She does not therefore choose independently; man sues, she chooses. But man's courtship is a question, and her choice only an answer to a question. In a certain sense, man is more than woman, in another sense he is infinitely less.[15]

"Seduction" means bringing the female spirit out of its vegetative state, and Johannes uses love letters to reach this goal, letters that he calls "clandestine communications."

> My letters do not fail their purpose. They develop her mentally, if not erotically. For that purpose I must not use letters but notes. The more the erotic is to come out, the shorter they should be, but the more positively they should stress the erotic side. However, in order not to make her sentimental or soft, irony must again stiffen her emotions, while yet giving her an appetite for the nourishment dearest to her. The notes vaguely and remotely suggest the absolute. As soon as this suspicion begins to dawn in her soul, the relation is ruptured.

> By my resistance the suspicion takes form in her
> soul, as if it were her own thought, her own heart's
> impulse. This is just what I want. 16

Woman's intimation of her own spirit appears in the guise of her thought; but this thought is actually his, claims Johannes. The psychological manifestation of spirit and love, in women, is anxiety, according to both Johannes and Vigilius. <u>Angst</u> betrays the female spirit. The only woman in history who has not betrayed anxiety, says Johannes, is Diana, the Greek goddess, who has remained virginal and untouched by suppressing anxiety in herself. This makes her a sort of female counterpart to Johannes, the Seducer. She controls herself, and he cannot manipulate her. The Seducer's idealization of Diana is an indication of his Madonna complex.

> When a girl has first given herself entirely, then
> everything is over. Always I approach a young girl
> with a certain anxiety, with a rapid pulse, because
> I feel the eternal power that lies in her nature.
> In the presence of a married woman I have never
> experienced it. The slight resistance she tries to
> offer with the help of art is nothing. It is as if
> one should say that a married woman's cap is more
> becoming than a young girl's uncovered head. For
> that reason Diana has always been my ideal. Her
> pure virginity, her absolute independence, has
> greatly engaged my attention. But while she has
> indeed occupied me, I have always kept a suspicious
> eye upon her. I imagine that she has not really
> deserved all the praise for her virginity that
> she has received. She knew that her role in life
> depended on her preserving her virginity. It

> happens that in a philological corner of the
> world, I have heard mumblings that she had an
> idea of the terrible birth pains her mother
> had gone through, and this had frightened her.
> I cannot blame Diana. I only say with Euripides:
> I would rather go to war three times than to
> bear one child. I could not really fall in love
> with Diana, but I do not deny that I would give
> much for a conversation with her, for what I
> might call a heart to heart talk with her. She
> must be well versed in various kinds of tricks.
> Obviously my good Diana in one way or another
> possesses a knowledge which makes her far less
> naive even than Venus. I am not interested in
> spying on her in her bath, not at all, but I
> would like to spy on her with my questions. If
> I were stealing off to a rendezvous where I
> feared for my victory, then I would prepare
> myself, arm myself, set all the spirits of love
> in motion, by conversing with her. 17

The Seducer's tendency to speak in myths is one of the manifestations of the myth-making in his own life. He deceives and manipulates by creating an aura of myth and fairytale in all that he does. His world is one of fairytale, and women are seduced and enticed into it.

> Everything is symbol; I myself am a myth about
> myself, for is it not as a myth that I hasten to
> this meeting? Who I am has nothing to do with it.
> Everything finite and temporal is forgotten, only
> the eternal remains, the power of love, its
> longing, its happiness. Now my soul is attuned
> like a bent bow, now my thoughts lie ready like
> arrows in my quiver, not poisoned, and yet able
> to blend themselves with the blood. How vigorous
> is my soul, sound, happy, omnipresent like a god. -
> Her beauty was a gift of Nature. I give thee
> thanks, O wonderful Nature! Like a mother hast
> thou watched over her. Accept my gratitude for
> thy care. Unsophisticated was she. I thank you,

> you human beings, to whom she was indebted for
> this. Her development was my handiwork - soon I
> shall enjoy my reward. 18

"Everything is imagery, I myself am a myth about myself." The Seducer does not want to exist as a concrete human subject; he wants to exist in the manner of a work of art. Although he has made love and life into works of art, and although he is only partly free, he is instrumental in causing women to achieve self-consciousness; his reflection, however, is directed only towards other, not towards self. He has not chosen to become a self, and has, therefore, not yet become involved in the actions of a self in the real world.

C. Irony and Humor

Johannes Climacus is Kierkegaard's pseudonym in Conclusive Unscientific Postscript (1846). Climacus interprets the ethical stage as follows:

> From an ethical point of view, reality is higher than possibility. The ethical wants precisely to annihilate possibility, which is without interest, by making existence infinitely interesting. The ethical, therefore, wants to prevent any attempts at creating confusion, as for example the attempt to observe the world and human beings ethically. For it is impossible to observe something ethically since there is only one kind of ethical observation, which is self-observation. The ethical immediately encircles the individual, demanding that he exist ethically; the ethical is not concerned with the masses and generations, or with mankind in general,

> just as it would be unthinkable for the police
> to arrest all of mankind. The ethical is concerned
> with the individual, indeed with each single person.
> Just as God knows the number of hairs on a person's
> head, so too does the ethical know how many human
> beings exist, and the ethical census is not inter-
> ested in the total, but in the individual. The
> ethical claims itself in every single human being,
> and it judges each one of them; only tyrants and
> impotent individuals are content to decimate. The
> ethical seizes the individual and requires him to
> refrain from all observation, especially of the
> world and of human beings; for the ethical, which
> is internal, cannot be observed from the outside by
> anyone; it can only be realized by the individual
> subject who in this way becomes aware of what is
> inherent in himself: that is, the only reality which
> does not become a possibility by being known, and
> which cannot be known merely by being thought,
> since it is his own reality which he knew as
> reality by thinking it, i.e., as possibility,
> before it turned into reality; whereas he could
> know nothing about the reality of another human
> being until he thought it by learning about it,
> i.e., changed it into possibility. (J.V.) 19

For the person in the ethical stage, reality is higher than possibility; he does not reflect upon other, but upon himself. The ethical life is realized only by the individual subject, by his questioning his own reality. The aesthete relates to the ideal as something external to himself; to the ethical individual, ideality is derived from internal self. Reality as pure possibility is the poetic word, and the mythical; concrete reality is action:

> Compared to possibility, the word is the highest
> pathos; compared to reality, action is the highest
> pathos. The fact that a poet, for example, is not
> affected by his own poetic creation, is aestheti-
> cally quite all right; or rather, it makes no
> difference, for poetic creation and possibility
> are the highest from an aesthetic point of view.
> The opposite is true from an ethical point of
> view; for the poetic work is without any ethical
> value whatsoever, but the poet's own existence
> must be infinitely more important to him than
> anything else. Aesthetically it would be the
> highest pathos for the poet to annihilate himself,
> to become demoralized if need be, in order to
> create a work of the highest order; aesthetically
> it is right to sell one's soul to the Devil (I
> am using strong language to call to mind a deed
> done more often than one would think) - and then
> work miracles. Ethically it might be the highest
> pathos to renounce the shining life of the poet.
> When a so-called religious individual depicts
> eternal bliss under the spell of imagination,
> then we have a poet who has deserted the aesthetical,
> and who wants to be naturalized in the religious
> without even understanding the native tongue. The
> pathos of the ethical is to act. (J.V.) 20

Poetic pathos, which we find examples of in the aesthetic stage, depends upon the de-personalization of the individual, the objectification of the subject; ethical pathos is a manifestation of the concrete human subject who acts in the real world. The ethical individual relates ironically to the world:

> Irony is the unity of ethical passion, which
> sincerely and infinitely accentuates the Self
> in relation to the ethical demand - and

> sophistication, which abstracts infinitely
> from Self in relation to the outside world,
> and which makes the Self finite like all
> other finite particulars. This abstraction
> means that no one notices the former (ethical
> passion), and that is the essence of this art;
> in this way the former is made truly infinite.
> (J.V.) 21

The world is something which the ethical individual knows he is not; irony becomes his medium. His irony is infinite seriousness paradoxically unified with its own opposite - the finite, the superficial, the un-serious. Irony can be defined as the <u>incognito</u> of the ethical subject.

> But why does the ethical individual use
> irony as his incognito? Because he understands
> the contradiction between the way in which he
> exists in his innermost Self and the fact that
> he does not express this Self outwardly; for
> it is true that the ethical individual reveals
> himself in so far as he is engaged in the
> tasks of real life, but so is the unsophisti-
> cated individual; what makes him an ethical
> individual is the process by which he coordinates
> his external and internal life in accordance
> with the infinite demand of the ethical, and
> this is not obvious. In order not to be disturbed
> by the finite, by all relative things in the world,
> the ethical individual places the comical between
> himself and the world, thus ensuring that he does
> not become comical himself due to a naive misunder-
> standing of his ethical passion. (J.V.) 22

The same relationship exists between humor and the religious individual:

> Religiousness with humor as its incognito is
> therefore: the unity of absolute (i.e., made
> genuine by a dialectical process) religious
> passion and spiritual maturity, which makes
> religiousness abstain from any superficial dis-
> play of sincerity, and that is in itself a mani-
> festation of absolute religious passion. The
> religious individual discovers that what occupies
> him in an absolute sense engages others only
> minimally; he concludes nothing from this fact,
> however, partly because he does not have the time
> for it, and partly because he cannot know for sure
> that all these individuals are not true knights of
> secret sincerity; the world around him prompts him
> to do that which his own dialectical sincerity re-
> quires of him: to erect a secret wall between himself
> and others in order to protect and safeguard the
> sincerity of suffering and religiousness. It does
> not follow from this, though, that such a religious
> individual becomes inactive; on the contrary, he
> does not absent himself from the world, but remains
> in it, for remaining in it is precisely his
> incognito. (J.V.) 23

Humor is the incognito of the religious subject, a self-protective method by which he conceals his own seriousness and his sincerity (<u>Inderlighed</u>) from a world that is insincere. This relationship between humor and religiousness, and between irony and the ethical mode of life, is a free one, chosen by the individual, not in order to obscure himself, but to preserve his freedom of action vis-a-vis other human beings. The ethical and religious personalities exist and act in the world through the incognito of irony and humor; they reveal themselves freely in the incognito, whereas the incognito of the demonic personality is a function of unfreedom, of the fear to become free. The dialectical progression from aesthetic freedom, which is unconsciously free, to the self-conscious stage of freedom in the ethical and religious stages, is also a progression from the particular, the finite (which can be the product of <u>unconscious freedom</u> in the aesthete, or of <u>conscious unfreedom</u> in the demonic) to the universal, or general, which is the ethical stage. The ethical demand is the demand to realize oneself in action, thus becoming part of the world in general. The synthesis of the individual or particular and the general or universal is posited as spirit; but the religious stage is an even further and more profound realization of concrete subjectivity; the religious subject relates to other as to another subject (that other subject which is God, from a theological point of view). The religious category is the realization of the absolute; it is transcendental and comes to the individual in the form of the absurd. Johannes Climacus says about the absurd:

> What is, now, the absurd? The absurd is that eternal truth has come into existence in time, that God has come into existence, has been born, has grown up, etc.; that he has developed completely like a human being and is not to be distinguished from another human being; for all immediate recognition is pre-socratic hedonism and worship of false gods from the point of view of Judaism; and any deter-

> mination of that which goes beyond the socratic
> way of thinking must denote its relation to God's
> existence, because the gradual development of
> faith, sensu strictissimo, also denotes this
> relation. Socrates' belief in the existence of
> God entailed a recognition of the fact that
> objective approximation - through observation of
> nature and history, for example - is a deviation
> from the way to God. He deserves recognition for
> having avoided this deviation, where the quanti-
> fying siren's song bewitches and tricks the
> individual. Compared to the absurd, objective
> approximation is like the comedy of successive
> misunderstandings commonly performed by private
> tutors and profiteers. (J.V.) 24

The paradoxical nature of the absurd is derived from the unity of eternal truth and concrete, subjective existence.

> Subjectivity is truth. This paradox was born because
> eternal, essential truth was related to the individual.
> Let us continue now; let us assume that eternal, es-
> sential truth itself is the paradox. How is this para-
> dox created? By combining eternal, essential truth
> and existence. Since truth itself is a combination
> of these two, truth becomes a paradox. Eternal truth
> came into existence in time. This is the paradox. If
> the human subject immediately prior to this was pre-
> vented by sin from regaining himself in eternity, he
> should not be worried about it any more; for eternal,
> essential truth is not behind him now; it is in front
> of him by existing or having existed in itself; so,
> if the individual does not grasp truth by existing,
> through existence, he will never have it. (J.V.) 25

The eternal exists in _time_, and the individual relates to it in time, in _history_, through the realization of his own spirit. Irony and humor are ways of relating to the temporal and the eternal, methods by which the two are mediated, unified, in individual life. The aesthete relates to the world through objective reflection only, whereas the ethical and religious individual relates through subjective reflection. Subjective reflection establishes a historical identity in the life of the individual; it creates continuity through recollection, which in Kierkegaard's terminology is something else than memory. Memory recalls only isolated, non-continuous moments; recollection recalls and synthesizes events into a continuous totality, a personal identity which preserves itself through the dialectical function of irony.

Kierkegaard's own creativity as a religious writer can be clarified if we take the ironic perspective into account; Kierkegaard creates synthesis dialectically, as the logical, psychological and existential progression from the aesthetical to the ethical and religious. Irony is the methodology by which the stages are contrasted to each other and dialectically subsumed under one another. Irony becomes an instrument of self-consciousness, a tool which divides and polarizes the stages; and a tool which simultaneously unifies the stages by showing how one is related to another through logical necessity; the logically necessary turns into the existentially free in Kierkegaard's philosophy, because the dialectic depends upon concrete, individual choice.

Irony is Søren Kierkegaard's own incognito, his pseudonym, through which he *is* and *is* *not*; he tells the truth through lying, emphasizing a point by identifying himself with the contrasting position. Kierkegaard saw that he had to bring out the truth slowly, and this entailed assuming the guise of a literary seducer who points to all the positive sides of the aesthetic life, initially, only to negate and discard that life in the next breath. The aesthete can, in this manner, be seduced or induced into the ethical and religious. The process is an internal, subjective one as well as an objective logical one. Self-consciousness is slowly achieved through reflection and persuasion. Reflection is directed towards the unconsciously free as well as towards the consciously unfree, the demonic. Kierkegaard's objective as an author is to bring out that reality which has been suppressed in un-reality; he achieves this objective by making the individual relate to time and change, by making him instigate his own dynamic growth so that he can be part of history by <u>becoming</u>. The unconsciously free and the consciously unfree are static modes of existence; but history means becoming; it means future time, that time which is the moment (<u>Øieblikket</u>) where the synthesis of the temporal and the eternal is posited.

Kierkegaard uses irony, then, as a contrasting technique; he poses as something he is not, retaining and suspending his awareness of what he is for the sake of persuading the individual to choose himself as a concrete subject. The object of Kierkegaard's persuasion ideally achieves Kierkegaard's own level of insight, and this subtle process relates the Danish philosopher to Modernism. Kierkegaard uses a language which de-mystifies, a dialectic of de-mystification. The objective of this dialectic is to bring a suppressed or unconscious reality out into the open, to reveal it. In modernist literature, that suppressed reality speaks its own mystified and mystifying language, perhaps the language of conscious unfreedom, demonic shut-upness, <u>indesluttethed</u>. But the relationship of Modernism to its own introversion is ironic because the enclosed consciousness strives to emancipate itself while at the same time realizing its own state of unemancipation.

Freedom is, curiously and obscurely, disguised as unfreedom, the state of mind that has closed itself off but yet relates to freedom. Kierkegaard interprets the demonic as having lost freedom; the human subject, in modernity, is unfree, imprisoned, for a variety of personal and social reasons, and must move in intricate ways to become free and to produce freedom in action.[26]

CHAPTER I REFERENCES

[1] Søren Kierkegaard, *The Concept of Anxiety*, trans. Reidar Thomte (Princeton, N.J: Princeton University Press, 1980), pp. 43-44.

[2] Kierkegaard, p. 85.

[3] Kierkegaard, p. 89.

[4] Kierkegaard, pp. 90-91.

[5] Kierkegaard, pp. 48-49.

[6] I am not concerned with Kierkegaard's theological explications of original sin here; but I *am* concerned with the implication and effect of original sin, i.e., estrangement from spirit.

[7] Kierkegaard, p. 61.

[8] Kierkegaard, p. 64.

[9] In the next part of this chapter, I shall discuss how and why the Seducer regards women as not determined by spirit.

[10] Kierkegaard, p. 119.

[11] Kierkegaard, p. 123.

[12] Kierkegaard, p. 124.

[13] Kierkegaard, p. 128.

[14] Søren Kierkegaard, Samlede Vaerker, Bd. 7. (København: Gyldendal, 1963), pp. 71-72.

[15] Søren Kierkegaard, Either-Or, trans. David F. Swenson and Lillian Marvin Swenson (Garden City, New York: Anchor Books, 1959), p. 426.

[16] Kierkegaard, Either-Or, p. 392.

[17] Kierkegaard, Either-Or, pp. 430-431.

[18] Kierkegaard, Either-Or, p. 439.

[19] Søren Kierkegaard, Samlede Vaerker, Bd. 10. (København: Gyldendal, 1963), pp. 25-26.

[20] Kierkegaard, Bd. 10, pp. 84-85.

[21] Kierkegaard, Bd. 10, p. 180.

[22] Kierkegaard, Bd. 10, p. 181.

[23] Kierkegaard, Bd. 10, pp. 182-183.

[24] Søren Kierkegaard, Samlede Vaerker, Bd. 9. (København: Gyldendal, 1963), pp. 175-176.

[25] Kierkegaard, Bd. 9, p. 174.

[26] I shall examine this complex process in my discussion of the novels.

CHAPTER 2

SEXUALITY AND COMMUNICATION ACCORDING TO FREUD

A.   The Libido Theory

As we have seen, Kierkegaard emphasized the importance of sexuality in his analysis of human consciousness; according to the Danish philosopher, sexual maturation was conducive to self-consciousness as well as to the positing of the male-female dualism. Sexual consciousness was a prerequisite for the self-consciousness of the spirit in human beings, and at the same time it was the cause of a division which estranged humanity from the spirit, and which introduced guilt and original sin.

A presentation of Sigmund Freud's psychology and meta-psychology will elucidate the role played by sexuality in the maturation process and in the organization of human consciousness. Freud's libido theory forms a structural model which describes and interprets the developmental stages in life; it is also a model which defines and organizes the distribution of libidinal energy throughout the various psychic systems or agencies, the id, the ego, and the super-ego. The first stage of sexual development, the pre-genital stage, is an auto-erotic stage divided into an oral phase and an anal phase, during which the object of erotic stimulation is the subject's own body. The sexual instincts, which originate in the undifferentiated id, are not directed towards external objects at this stage, as the child (before age three) does not clearly distinguish objects outside his body; they are incorporated into his mental life without signifying a clearly separate, external world. The oral and anal phases are followed by a phallic or Oedipal phase during which the child searches for an external object of his libidinal impulses; the primary object of these libidinal impulses is the mother, in the case of male children. The male child has to compete with the father for the mother, which leads to an Oedipal conflict, resulting in the repression or inhibition of the libido. This forced repression of the libido produces hatred of the father, a death-wish against him; already at this point, i.e., before the development of a differentiated ego, an ego which is separate from the id, Freud observes the presence of two conflicting instincts in the id, the sexual instincts and the death instincts. The Oedipal conflict, or the "Oedipus complex", is overcome through de-sexualization of the sexual desire for the mother; the child's incipient wish to establish genital primacy through object-choice is thus thwarted and inhibited, and the process of de-sexualization is extended into the latency period (age six to eight). After the period of latency, the child, or adolescent, re-initiates his search for a love-object; if the maturation process is normal, this object becomes another female, not his mother, and the adolescent is able to progress to the genital stage and to subsequent maturity. In order to accomplish this development, the child must detach his libidinal wishes from the mother-figure, and he must also liberate himself from any subservience to the father-figure, reconcile himself with him and become a mature adult in his own right.

The arrival of the genital stage in the developmental process signals the birth of a differentiated ego, which is separate from the id, and which is conscious of reality and necessity. In the ego, the sexual instincts are modified and balanced against the ego-instincts, the instincts of self-preservation which must give in to the demands of reality. Freud points to a central dualism in the organization of human mental life, the pleasure principle and the reality principle. The pleasure principle is a system which aims at the gratification of libidinal instincts; the reality principle is a system which aims at making the ego recognize reality and necessity.

The ego does not, however, exclude libidinal instincts; it contains sexuality, and its sexuality is not qualitatively different from that of the id; sexuality, or libidinal energy, is distributed topographically, and is equally present in both agencies. The ego is thus divided between the attainment of pleasure and the reality-given preservation of self. Libidinal energy is also distributed between the ego and objects; ego-cathexis is the charging of the ego itself with libido, which produces narcissism; object-cathexis is the "normal" charging of external objects with libido. Narcissism in the infantile stage is called primary narcissism, also called auto-erotism. The adult person may develop tendencies which reflect the stages of primary narcissism, neurotic tendencies the main symptom of which is an inability to distinguish reality. In the adult, such a neurosis creates a debilitating lack of communication with reality and other people; ego-cathexis produces a secondary narcissism. The detachment of libido from external objects is closely related to repression and fixation and may result in a complete regression to the stage of primary narcissism. Narcissistic libido is thus a symptom of an arrested, or fixated, maturation process by which the individual regresses to an earlier developmental stage.

Freud's libido theory operates with bound and unbound libidinal energy. Sexual and ego-instincts are bound, to an extent, in object-cathexis and ego-cathexis, but there is a quantity of free-flowing libido present in the psyche. Unbound libido reduces the ego's ability to adjust to reality, and the libido surplus must be repressed or diverted; the psyche, therefore, creates a third agency, the ego-ideal, also called conscience or super-ego. This agency operates as a critical censor; it is a self-observing faculty which prevents the unbound libido from erupting, from disturbing the balance of the psyche. The normal functioning of the psyche depends upon the distribution of libido energy throughout the unconscious and conscious agencies, and the satisfaction of libidinal instincts is relative to the control of the ego which strives to channelize the libido in accordance with the reality principle.

B. The Life and Death Instincts

In two of his later works, Beyond the Pleasure Principle (1920) and Civilization and its Discontents (1930), Freud reiterates his analysis of how libido energy is distributed among the psychic agencies, and speculates on the pattern of distribution related to human culture and civilization at large. These works are meta-psychological in content, because they go beyond psychological interpretation in an attempt to theorize about psychological and social relationships on a philosophical level. Freud theorizes about the meaning of pleasure and unpleasure:

> We have decided to relate pleasure and unpleasure to the quantity of excitation that is present in the mind but is not in any way 'bound'; and to relate them in such a manner that unpleasure corresponds to an *increase* in the quantity of excitation and pleasure to a *diminution*. What we are implying by this is not a simple relation between the strength of the feelings of pleasure and unpleasure and the corresponding modifications in the quantity of excitation; least of all -- in view of all we have been taught by psycho-physiology -- are we suggesting any directly proportional ratio: the factor that determines the feeling is probably the amount of increase or diminution in the quantity of excitation *in a given period of time.* [1]

Pleasure and unpleasure have a psycho-physical relation to conditions of stability and instability. The human mind is basically conservative and wants to preserve a status quo; the mental apparatus has a proclivity towards preserving an equilibrium. Disrupting the equilibrium produces unpleasure, pain; achieving constancy and balance thus involves obediance to the pleasure principle, which strives to reduce the influx of stimuli to a level that is tolerable to the ego. The pleasure principle co-operates with the reality principle; achieving stability involves not only the gratification of libidinal impulses, but also the postponement of gratification. The ego is expanded, in Freud's later works, to include both conscious and unconscious material, and the ego - which is bent upon avoiding unpleasure - resists the release of material that has been repressed into the unconscious. This resistance manifests itself as a compulsion to repeat, i.e., to remain in a repressive pattern of behavior rather than liberating painful unconscious material. The ego would be able to tolerate the release of painful material if the mental apparatus could adjust itself to change, which always involves a certain degree of unpleasure. Freud is confronted with a paradox here: much of the repressed material is, and was originally, painful in itself, and yet the release of it is regarded as even more painful by the ego. It becomes difficult to regard the compulsion to repeat as a mental activity designed to promote pleasure; but it is, nonetheless, an activity by which the ego achieves a degree of mastery over a situation, in that repressed material, through the symbolic re-enactment of an originally painful childhood experience, is translated into a symptomatic behavior pattern; this behavior pattern consists in actions that revolve around the same experience and repeat that experience in a modified form in an effort to control it. The compulsion to repeat, Freud speculates, is evidence of a conservative instinct that is inherent in nature:

> At this point we cannot escape a suspicion that we may have come upon the track of a universal attribute of instincts and perhaps of organic life in general which has not hitherto been clearly recognized or at least not explicitly stressed. *It seems, then, that an instinct is an urge inherent in organic life to restore an earlier state of things* which the living entity has been obliged to abandon under the pressure of external disturbing forces; that is, it is a kind of organic elasticity, or, to put it another way, the expression of the inertia inherent in organic life.
> This view of instincts strikes us as strange because we have become used to see in them a factor impelling towards change and development, whereas we are now asked to recognize in them the precise contrary — an expression of the *conservative* nature of living substance.[2]

The conservative instinct compels towards repetition, while other instincts produce progress and new forms; the compulsion to repeat becomes synonymous with an instinctive impulse, inherent in all organic life, to return to the inorganic state; instinctual life as a whole serves to bring about death. The instinct of self-preservation and the instinct to achieve mastery are component instincts whose function it is to make sure that the organism follows its own path towards death; they are death-instincts.

By contrast, the sexual instincts are life-instincts; they produce new forms and change in the life of the individual and the species. Freud's name for the life-instinct is Eros; the ego partakes of Eros since it has libidinal energy attached to it. Freud rejects his own previous assumption that there was a clear dualism in the psyche between sexual instincts and ego-instincts. A portion of the ego-instincts is libidinal, since, as we have seen, Freud's theory of narcissism involved the ego-cathexis of libido energy. Sexual instincts operate in the ego; hence the death-instincts cannot be equated exclusively with ego-instincts. The ego, as well as the id, are the vehicles of a new dualism, the life-death dualism. There is an opposition in the entire psychic organism between the life and death instincts. The death instincts which are primarily associated with the compulsion to repeat, i.e., to regress to an earlier form of mental life, are also associated with aggression and destructiveness; the psychological manifestations of aggression and destructiveness are sexual variants, or deviations, sadism and masochism.

In his meta-psychological works, Freud abstracts from the internal mental life of deviants and speculates about the expressions of aggression in civilization; he proceeds from the biological to the cultural repressions of the death instincts and the sexual instincts. His theory of the origin of sexuality takes him back to Plato's *Symposium*,[3] where Aristophanes states that, originally, human nature was different from what it is now; there were three sexes, man, woman, and the union of the two. These primeval humans were double: they had four hands and four feet, two faces, two genitals, etc. Zeus eventually decided to cut these beings in half, after which the two parts of man, each desiring his other half, came together, eager to grow into one again. The impetus which propels the two halves towards each other is the sexual instinct, or life instinct, whose objective it is to reunite life, create a synthesis out of the fragments of life.

Freud's evolving theory of the life and death instincts is congruent with his changing perception of how libido energy is distributed among the psychic agencies.

He sums up his theory as follows:

> ... our enquiries advanced from the repressed to the repressing forces, from the object-instincts to the ego. The decisive step forward was the introduction of the concept of narcissism -- that is to say, the discovery that the ego itself is cathected with the libido, that the ego, indeed, is the libido's original home, and remains to some extent its headquarters. This narcissistic libido turns towards objects, and thus becomes object-libido; and it can change back into narcissistic libido once more. The concept of narcissism made it possible to obtain an analytical understanding of the traumatic neuroses and of many of the affections bordering on the psychoses, as well as of the latter themselves. It was not necessary to give up our interpretation of the transference neuroses as attempts made by the ego to defend itself against sexuality; but the concept of libido was endangered. Since the ego-instincts, too, were libidinal, it seemed for a time inevitable that we should make libido coincide with instinctual energy in general, as C. G. Jung had already advocated earlier. Nevertheless, there still remained in me a kind of conviction, for which I was not as yet able to find reasons, that the instincts could not all be of the same kind. My next step was taken in *Beyond the Pleasure Principle* (1920g), when the compulsion to repeat and the conservative character of instinctual life first attracted my attention. Starting from speculations on the beginning of life and from biological parallels, I drew the conclusion that, besides the instinct to preserve living substance and to join it into ever larger units, there must exist another, contrary instinct seeking to dissolve those units and to bring them back to their primaeval, inorganic state. That is to say, as well as Eros there was an instinct of death.[4]

As we have noted, the manifestations of the death instinct are aggressiveness and destructiveness. This aggressiveness can be introjected, internalized, because of external obstacles to its expression, social and moral codes, etc.; aggression becomes directed towards the ego itself, and is taken over by the ego-ideal, or super-ego; this results in a punitive form of conscience. The tension between the aggressive super-ego and the ego that is subjected to it expresses itself as a sense of guilt and as a need for punishment. The individual conscience becomes a reflection or duplication of the moral institutions of civilization, institutions which require that the individual must renounce his instinctual wishes.

> Thus we know of two origins of the sense of guilt: one arising from fear of an authority, and the other, later on, arising from fear of the super-ego. The first insists upon a renunciation of instinctual satisfactions; the second, as well as doing this, presses for punishment, since the continuance of the forbidden wishes cannot be concealed from the super-ego. We have also learned how the severity of the super-ego -- the demands of conscience -- is to be understood. It is simply a continuation of the severity of the external authority, to which it has succeeded and which it has in part replaced. We now see in what relationship the renunciation of instinct stands to the sense of guilt. Originally, renunciation of instinct was the result of fear of an external authority: one renounced one's satisfactions in order not to lose its love. If one has carried out this renunciation, one is, as it were, quits with the authority and no sense of guilt should remain. But with fear of the super-ego the case is different. Here, instinctual renunciation is not enough, for the wish persists and cannot be concealed from the

> super-ego. Thus, in spite of the renunciation that has been made, a sense of guilt comes about. This constitutes a great economic disadvantage in the erection of a super-ego, or, as we may put it, in the formation of a conscience. Instinctual renunciation now no longer has a completely liberating effect; virtuous continence is no longer rewarded with the assurance of love. A threatened external unhappiness -- loss of love and punishment on the part of the external authority -- has been exchanged for a permanent internal unhappiness, for the tension of the sense of guilt.[5]

Freud's concept of the death instinct thus involves both aggression, guilt, and punishment; the death instinct, furthermore, operates in silence. Freud describes it as a mute energy:

> The manifestations of Eros were conspicuous and noisy enough. It might be assumed that the death instinct operated silently within the organism towards its dissolution, but that, of course, was no proof. A more fruitful idea was that a portion of the instinct is diverted towards the external world and comes to light as an instinct of aggressiveness and destructiveness. In this way the instinct itself could be pressed into the service of Eros, in that the organism was destroying some other thing, whether animate or inanimate, instead of destroying its own self. Conversely, any restriction of this aggressiveness directed outwards would be bound to increase the self-destruction, which is in any case proceeding. At the same time one can suspect from this example that the two kinds of instinct seldom -- perhaps never -- appear in isolation from each other, but are alloyed with each other in varying and very different proportions and so become unrecognizable to our judgement. In sadism, long since known to us as a component

> instinct of sexuality, we should have before
> us a particularly strong alloy of this kind
> between trends of love and the destructive
> instinct; while its counterpart, masochism,
> would be a union between destructiveness
> directed inwards and sexuality -- a union which
> makes what is otherwise an imperceptible trend
> into a conspicuous and tangible one.[6]

Paul Ricoeur states that there is a "disparity between the death instinct and its expressions, between desire and speech".[7] Psychoanalytic deciphering, the interpretation of psychic forces and symptoms, becomes difficult because of this disparity between "desire" and "speech". Complete deciphering is based on the equivalence of two systems of reference, instincts and meaning; in Freud's last works, only a partial deciphering occurs; the "silent operation" of the death instinct forces Freud into speculation and hypotheses, and these hypotheses require further elucidation; it is especially important to determine how the life and death instincts are related to each other, and whether libido energy is distributed between them. The meta-psychological works go through a transition from an old model, the ego, id, and super-ego, to a new model, a structural organization based upon the concept of the life and death instincts. The super-ego was seen to be derived from the Oedipal situation where the father-figure was internalized and transformed into an interior critical agent. Freud noted that super-ego could be cruel and punitive towards the ego; this observation led him to the theory that the super-ego was an extension of the death-instinct. Destructive energy became directed at the ego, which ensued in self-punishment and a sense of guilt, or perhaps unconscious moral sense.

The super-ego, therefore, must be interpreted as having an <u>instinctual</u> character; this relates the super-ego to the id, from where unbound and undifferentiated sexual and destructive energies flow. The ego, which partly obeys the reality principle, attempts to <u>defuse</u> the destructive energies, i.e., to convert them into neutral, displaceable energies which can be utilized for constructive purposes. In the economy of the mind's utilization of psychic energy, it is seen to be constructive to introject aggressive energy instead of directing it towards external objects; the cathexis of the super-ego with destructive energy takes place in accordance with the economics of energy management in the psyche; the death instinct must be defused in order not to be turned upon others; the defusion results in the introjection of the death-instinct. The destructiveness of the super-ego is, furthermore, coupled with libidinal residue from the Oedipal phase, during which the Oedipus complex, i.e., the child's sexual desire for his mother, was overcome by being de-sexualized, and by becoming latent. The residue of libido energy now manifests itself as a sadistic super-ego and contributes to the punitive nature of that agency. Paul Ricoeur notes that there is a difference between the sadism of the super-ego and the masochism of the ego; the sadism of the super-ego is an unconscious extension of morality, and although the super-ego contains a residue of libidinal energy, the critical agency was predominantly formed as a result of the process of de-sexualization; by contrast, the ego's desire for punishment expresses a <u>resexualization</u>:

> ... such a desire is connected with the wish to be beaten by the father, which we have seen to be one of the expressions of "erotogenic masochism." This desire expresses, therefore, a resexualization of morality, in the reverse direction of the normal movement of conscience and morality that arise from the overcoming and hence from the desexualization of the Oedipus complex. With the resexualization of morality the possibility of a monstrous fusion of love and death arises; such a fusion on the "sublime" plane has its counterpart on the "perverse" plane in the phenomena of pleasure in pain.
> One can see how dangerous it would be to confuse everything: normal morality, cruelty (the superego's sadism), need for punishment (the ego's masochism). These three tendencies-- the cultural suppression of the instincts, the turning back of sadism against the self, and the intensification of the ego's own masochism --

do indeed supplement each other and unite to
produce the same effects; but in principle at
least, they are distinct tendencies. The sense
of guilt results from a combination of these
tendencies in various proportions.[8]

The "erotogenic masochism" of the ego results in "a monstrous fusion of love and death", which can even become a pure culture of death:

> ... even if the sadism of the superego is
> independent of any erotic factor, we are
> presented with a view in which the death
> instinct is directly included in the sadism
> of the superego -- the result being what
> might be called a deathly sublimation. Such
> a view is suggested by the interrelating of
> defusion, desexualization, and sublimation.
> Thus the sadism of the superego represents
> a sublimated form of destructiveness; in
> proportion as destructiveness becomes de-
> sexualized by defusion, it becomes capable
> of being mobilized to the advantage of the
> superego; and at this point it becomes a
> "pure culture of death." The desexualization
> of sadism is therefore no less dangerous than
> the resexualization of masochism.[9]

The death instinct has now been elucidated somewhat, and it is deciphered even further; the instinct was originally seen to be a mute agent, but in the culture it expresses itself as the language of war:

> There is thus a progressive revelation of the
> death instinct at three levels, biological,
> psychological, cultural. Grasped at first
> in the complexities of Eros, the death instinct
> remained masked in the sadistic component;

> sometimes it reinforced object-libido, sometimes it hypercathected narcissistic libido; its antagonism becomes less and less silent as Eros develops, uniting living matter to itself, then the ego to its object, and finally individuals into ever wider groups. At this last level the struggle between Eros and Thanatos becomes declared war; paraphrasing Freud, one might say that war is the clamor of death.[10]

The "mute", but increasingly "clamoring" energy of the death-instinct finds a parallel expression in Kierkegaard's "fear of the good", the so-called demonic. The demonic is silent and has enclosed itself in itself, closed itself off from the good, i.e., the moral ideals of the culture and their representative in the psyche, the conscience. The demonic state manifests itself as fear of conscience, and the demonic category represents the furthest point of estrangement from spirit; the demonic shuns self-revelation; in the light of Freudian analysis, the demonic can be interpreted as being forced on to the devious intricate path of self-alienation and introversion by the operations of an ethical ideal which requires instinctual renunciation, the renunciation of sexuality. As we have seen, the death-instinct is diverted from external objects and injected into the psyche, where it acts as a sadistic super-ego, oppressing the ego which becomes the scene of the fusion of love and death. The fear of the good becomes a fear of the compulsion and impulsion to repress sexuality. Paradoxically, the demonic personality becomes unfree because it desires sexual freedom. In Kierkegaard's philosophy, becoming free means opening up to the universal, and the synthesis of the individual and the universal is based on the sublimation of sexuality. The demonic personality, whose prototype is Lucifer, is rebellious because it has resexualized the Oedipal conflict which, according to Freud, means that the Oedipus complex has not been overcome. This "rebellious" resexualization is counteracted and repressed by the aggressive moral agency, the conscience, which is the implicit father-figure that the "Luciferean" personality rebels against. The demonic mind is locked in a sado-masochistic pattern which it is compelled to repeat; seen from this point of view, the demonic category represents a regression to an earlier developmental stage, the Oedipal stage, which was never transcended. The problematic nature of the demonic personality, its psycho-pathological structure if you will, is derived from a deviant process of socialization. Hence Kierkegaard's description of the demonic as that which is forced to repeat the same tedious pattern; the demonic is unfreedom imprisoned in itself.

The demonic fear of conscience, and the aesthete's failure to recognize the meaning of the ethical life, have their social implications. The ethical ideal was deflated as it was embodied in the social vehicles of marriage and dutiful citizenship, ways of life which the aesthete found to be tedious and unfulfilling. The embodiment of the ethical ideal into mid-19th century bourgeois life style created a manifest tedium; the ethical ideal, which in itself was unrestricted, was subjected to social restrictions; both the demonic and the aesthetic personalities react against these restrictions, but also incorporate these same restrictions, ironically enough. The demonic mind represents an inversion of the ethical ideal, an inversion which is partly produced by the social perversion of that ideal; the demonic mind provides us with a distorted, but partly accurate and true reflection of social reality. The demonic and the aesthetic categories represent a refusal to adjust to and become integrated with 19th century middle class society; the aetiology of these categories can be derived from a sociological analysis of the discontinuity between subject and object. The individual realizes himself in relation to society and becomes free in relation to it; but society contains restrictions and represents a threat against the free development and expression of individual potential. Because of those social restrictions, the implicit nature of which is socioeconomic, the individual seeks self-realization in relation to the transcendental, or the meta-physical (a level which the demonic is alienated from, and which the aesthetic category anticipates in myth and poetry). The realization of individual freedom resolves the temporal, or social, discontinuity by transcending it, by creating a meta-physical continuity. The ethical ideal became conventionalized and deteriorated into a philistine moral code; Kierkegaard solved the problem by confronting the individual with an absolute ethical demand which subjectivized the value of the ideal by detaching it from its own function as conventional norm. Truth becomes subjective, and individual subjectivity is opposed absolutely to the world.

The aesthetic and demonic categories react to conventional reality in their own ways; the aesthete reacts by transforming his life into art, and the demonic mind engages in regression. The demonic is, in a way, an unconventional reflection or inversion of the conventional, the good turned into absence of good, empty ideality. The demonic fear of extroversion, the fear of self-revelation, is analogous to a pathological pattern of distorted communication.

C. Distorted Communication

Although I am not suggesting that the demonic and the pathological personalities are congruent, I believe that the distorted speech pattern we encounter in pathological patients is analogous to the private language, the speech of unfreedom, which is symptomatic of the demonic.

Freud dealt with deformed communication in order to define incomprehensible acts and utterances, as manifested in neurosis, psychosis, and psychosomatic disturbances, and applied his clinical insights to collective behavior and social systems. In an essay on "Systematically Distorted Communication", Jürgen Habermas discusses psychoanalysis as a linguistic analysis, and defines distorted communication:

> Three criteria are available for defining the scope of specific incomprehensible acts and utterances. (a) On the level of language, distorted communication becomes noticeable because of the use of rules which deviate from the recognized system of linguistic rules. Particularly semantical contents or complete semantical fields -- in extreme cases the syntax, too -- may be affected thereby. Using dream

texts, Freud examined, in particular, condensation, displacement, absence of proper use of grammar and the use of words with opposite meaning. (b) On the behaviour level, the deformed language-game appears in the form of rigidity and compulsory repetition. Stereotyped behaviour patterns recur in situations involving stimuli which cause emotionally loaded reactions. This inflexibility is symptomatic of the fact that the semantical content has lost its specific linguistic independence of the situational context. (c) If, finally, we consider the system of distorted communication as a whole, we are struck by the discrepancy between the levels of communication; the usual congruency between linguistic symbols, actions and accompanying gestures has disintegrated. The symptoms, in a clinical sense, offer nothing but the most recalcitrant and tangible proof of this dissonance. No matter on which level of communication the symptoms appear, whether in linguistic expression, in behavioural compulsion, or in the realm of gestures, one always finds an isolated content therein which has been excommunicated from the public language-performance. This content expresses an intention which is incomprehensible according to the rules of public communication, and which as such has become private, although in such a way that it remains inaccessible even to the author to whom is must, nevertheless, be ascribed. There is a communication obstruction in the self between the ego, which is capable of speech and participates in inter-subjectivity established language-games, and that 'inner foreign territory' (Freud), which is represented by a private or a primary linguistic symbolism.[11]

According to Kierkegaard, the demonic mind, which is unfree, communicates with freedom in spite of itself; freedom comes to it from the outside, trying to open it up. In the same manner, freedom , as analytical interpretation and scenic understanding, confronts and seeks to explicate the incomprehensible meaning of the patient's symptoms; the analyst creates a scene or situation of transference, where the patient forces the doctor into the role of the conflict-defined primary reference person. The doctor-patient scene parallels or repeats the symptomatic scene played by the patient outside the doctor's office, and it also parallels the original conflict-ridden situation experienced in childhood. The doctor's objective is to decode the meaning of the symptoms and relate it to the childhood experience.

> The re-established original scene is typically a situation in which the child has once suffered and repulsed an unbearable conflict. This repulse is coupled with a process of desymbolization and the formation of a symptom. The child excludes the experience of the conflict-filled object from public communication (and at the same time makes it inaccessible to its own ego as well); it separates the conflict-laden portion of its memory of the object and, so to speak, desymbolizes the meaning of the relevant reference person. The gap which arises in the semantic field is then closed by employing an unquestionable symbol in place of the isolated symbolic content. This symbol, of course, strikes us as being a symptom, because it has gained private linguistic significance and can no longer be used according to the rules of public language.[12]

The doctor's primary goal is to achieve or make the patient accomplish resymbolization, i.e., the re-entry of isolated, private symbolic contents into public communication. Scenic understanding makes it possible to translate the pathologically frozen communication pattern, thus making it accessible to public communication, and the doctor-patient scene is guided by a set of analytical rules and theoretical propositions concerning normal communication and distorted communication.

In the case of non-deformed communication, there is congruence between linguistic expressions, actions, and gestures; normal communication is public; the speakers are aware of the difference between subject and object, private and public; during normal communication, mutual understanding, guaranteeing ego-identity, is developed between individuals who recognize one another; people communicate on the basis of linguistic inter-subjectivity.

Distorted communication patterns are attributed to the confusion of two consecutive phases of pre-linguistic and linguistic symbol-organization; this confusion may be due to deviant socialization, i.e., abnormal patterns of behavior and interaction in childhood. Pre-linguistic symbol-organizations, the palaeo-symbols of speech, are only available to us through the analysis of dream material and speech pathology. Palaeo-symbols do not follow grammatical rules, they are emotionally loaded, and remain fixed to particular scenes; private meaning-associations prevail; objects and classes of objects are not categorized and identified. The mental operation whose sign is speech disorder, i.e., a palaeo-symbolic language pattern, is repression, or inhibition, and the function of the analyst is to achieve the re-symbolization of desymbolized, or inhibited language:

> The performance of the analyst in putting an end to the process of inhibition serves the purpose of resymbolization; inhibition itself can therefore be understood as a process link to desymbolization. The defence mechanism of inhibition, which is analogous to flight, is revealed by the patient in his resistance to plausible interpretations made by the analyst. This mechanism is an operation carried on with and by language; otherwise it would not be possible to reverse the process of repulsion hermeneutically, i.e. precisely by means of a special type of semantic analysis. The fleeing ego, which has to submit to the demands of outer reality in a conflict situation, hides itself from itself by eliminating the symbolic representation of unwanted demands of instinct from the text of its everyday consciousness. By means of this censorship the representation of the prohibited object is excommunicated from public communication and banished to the archaic level of palaeo-symbols. Moreover, the assumption that neurotic behaviour is controlled by palaeo-symbols, and only subsequently rationalized by a substitutive interpretation, offers an explanation for the characteristics of this behaviour pattern: for its pseudo-communicative function, for its stereotyped and compulsive form, for its emotional load and expressive content, and, finally, for its rigid fixation upon particular situations.[13]

The analytical scene facilitates the creative extension of language whereby palaeo-symbolic meaning-potential is made available for public communication, and this "transfer of semantic contents from the pre-linguistic into the common stock of language widens the scope of communicative action as it diminishes that of unconsciously motivated action. The moment of success in the use of creative language is a moment of emancipation."[14]

The pre-linguistic symbol-organization of distorted speech, and the ego which hides from itself, parallels the fear of self-revelation, the fear to become integrated into public communication; the difference is, of course, that the neurotic patient is totally unconscious of the nature of his disorder, whereas the demonic mind, according to Kierkegaard, consciously excludes the dimension of freedom; but like the pathological mind, the demonic mind remains fixed in a compulsive pattern of repetition and regression by which meaning is desymbolized, rendered meaningless. The demonic is that which is excommunicated.

The aesthete, by contrast, extends language creatively; this extension functions, initially, as a poeticizing and a mythification of reality, and as a consciousness of other, a reflective activity which renders its unconscious object conscious of itself; and consciousness of other is followed by self-consciousness and self-emancipation.

CHAPTER II REFERENCES

[1] Sigmund Freud, *Complete Psychological Works*, Vol. 18, (London: The Hogarth Press, 1955) pp. 7-8.

[2] Freud, *Psychological Works*, p. 36.

[3] Freud, *Psychological Works*, p. 57ff.

[4] Sigmund Freud, *Civilization and its Discontents*. (New York: W.W. Norton & Company, 1962) pp. 65-66.

[5] Freud, *Civilization*, pp. 74-75.

[6] Freud, *Civilization*, p. 66.

[7] Paul Ricoeur, *Freud and Philosophy*. (New Haven: Yale University Press, 1970) p. 294.

[8] Ricoeur, *Freud*, pp. 300-301.

[9] Ricoeur, *Freud*, pp. 301-302.

[10] Ricoeur, *Freud*, p. 306.

[11] Jürgen Habermas, "Systematically Distorted Communication." In *Critical Sociology*, Paul Connerton, Ed. (New York: Penguin Books, 1976) pp. 349-350.

[12] Habermas, p. 351.

[13] Habermas, p. 358.

[14] Habermas, p. 359.

CHAPTER 3

HERMENEUTICS AND THE CREATIVE
PROCESS - HUNGER

My interpretation of Knut Hamsun's novel Hunger (1890) is based on hermeneutics and its relationship, as an interpretive device, to Marxist and Modernist aesthetics. My preliminary position is that hermeneutics can serve as a mediating link between Marxism and Modernism; by means of such a link, I can bring Kierkegaard's philosophy into a more direct relationship to Marxism and Modernism and indicate some structural parallels between Kierkegaard's definition of perceptual consciousness and the aesthetic imagination, the concept of literary form, as it is conceptualized in the two apparently contrasting systems of Marxist and Modernist thought.

The Marxist theoretical system sees all branches of human knowledge and culture as related to a societal, historical totality; the development of separate sciences and arts may be independent, but is ultimately related to the historical process through a dialectic which points to everything's interrelation with everything else, namely dialectical materialism. The pseudo-Marxist perception of dialectic is that the economic base is the primary cause of the products of consciousness as they are shaped in the so-called superstructure. Real Marxism, however, denies such a mechanical aetiology. Dialectical materialism is a dynamic, kinetic dialectic which makes manifest the interrelationship between all phenomena of life and culture, and which expresses and reveals the progressive change of phenomena and their relation to human and historical essence, i.e., the natural and total integration of the various areas of human endeavor. A realistic, scientific explanation of the changes and developments that occur within each separate branch of science and art would see these changes as the specific forms and manifestations of general change which follows a pattern of universal rules governing the process of evolution in society. Marxism does not deny the fact that art and science can evolve independently of the material base, but Marxist ideology does reject the idea that the development of art and science is immanent rather than historical. The aesthetic nature of literary works is part of a general, interrelated societal process through which the human subject absorbs, assimilates, and makes the world real through consciousness; but this consciousness does not follow the changes of economic production mechanistically; it often contradicts these changes. Art forms

are not the mere reflection of the forms of production;
art may anticipate new forms of production and new class
relationships. Marxist philosophy emphasizes the important role of individual creative energy and activity
throughout history; the human being creates itself, makes
itself human. The very nature of independent human activity in the various productive spheres has an objective
aetiology which is both individual and historical, particular and universal. At some points in history, e.g.
the Renaissance, art was integrated in the total human
sphere of work; at other points, e.g. under Capitalism,
art seems to be dissociated from the societal totality.
This apparent dissociation is due to the division of
labor, according to Marx, a division which was produced
by industrial Capitalism; specialization ensued, and the
various human spheres of labor were divorced from one
another. The dissociation of art in Modernity is only
apparent, in my point of view, for the objective of art
is still to express the natural integration of the human
subject with the culture it is a part of; it is the precise purpose of dialectical materialism to re-structure
the perceptual process of human consciousness by informing
it with a cultural ideal, a *negative*, which constructively
and concretely negates the division of labor and con-

sciousness. This negation is achieved through the cognition of the relativity of phenomena and their relation to essence, i.e., integrated being. The human totality is revealed through a dialectical analysis of economics and art, an interpretative process which uncovers the apparent divisions and separations and relativizes them, i.e., recognizes them as social phenomena, not absolute ontological concepts. Contrary to Lukacs, for example, I contend that Modernism, as a cognitive system of thought and as a literary vehicle, expresses these relative divisions as well as their potential negation and integration. Such a point of view utilizes Marxist aesthetic theory kinetically, not statically or mechanistically.

As I have indicated, dialectical thought sees the evolution of ideological history as being irregular and not simply correlated to the material base. The economically highest step in the evolution of class society is Capitalism, but the conditions for literature and art under Capitalism are unfavorable, according to Marx. Marx's economic theory comprehends and analyzes the categories of being as relations between human subjects and as relations between nature and society. Under Capitalism, natural relations are obfuscated, fetichized. The world is perceived to be different from what it really is; it is distorted and reified in human consciousness, and art and literature must, consequently, make an effort to see through this fetichism by interpreting and making manifest the real essence behind the surface phenomena of social reality. Marx describes fetichism primarily as a result of the conversion of use-value to exchange-value through the capitalist production process, a process whereby the real use-value of a commodity and the labor inherent in it, is transformed to exchange-value and surplus-value, whereby profit is created as the unequal valorization of labor; labor, in other words, is exchanged for a commodity which has more monetary value than the human work put into it, and commodities are exchangeable for all other commodities and are thus imbued with pseudo-independent life on the marketplace.

> A commodity is therefore a mysterious thing, simply because in it the social character of men's labor appears to them as an objective character stamped upon the product of that labor: because the relation of the producers to the sum total of their own labour is presented to them as a social relation, existing not between themselves, but between the products of their labour. This is the reason why the products of labour become commodities, social things whose qualities are at the same time perceptible and imperceptible by the senses. In the same way the light from an object is perceived by us not as the subjective excitation of our optic nerve, but as the objec-

tive form of something outside the eye itself. But, in the act of seeing, there is at all events, an actual passage of light from one thing to another, from the external object to the eye. There is a physical relation between physical things. But it is different with commodities. There, the existence of the things *qua* commodities, and the value-relation between the products of labour which stamps them as commodities, have absolutely no connexion with their physical properties and with the material relations arising therefrom. There it is a definite social relation between men, that assumes, in their eyes, the fantastic form of a relation between things. In order, therefore, to find an analogy, we must have recourse to the mist-enveloped regions of the religious world. In that world the productions of the human brain appear as independent beings endowed with life, and entering into relation both with one another and the human race. So it is in the world of commodities with the products of men's hands. This I call the Fetishism which attaches itself to the products of labour, so soon as they are produced as commodities, and which is therefore inseparable from the production of commodities.[1]

Social relations exist, now, between the commodities themselves rather than between human beings, which creates reification, i.e., the false perception that social relations are analogous to the relations among things. Phenomena are divorced from human essence, and the private subject becomes a commodity in itself; creative products are exchanged on the marketplace where money is the universal whore, and the artist himself is forced to enter into a reified relationship with his audience. Literature must both reflect and contradict this relationship under

Capitalism, and for this reason the conditions under which art is produced are more difficult and complex than during earlier periods. The literary work as a reflection of external reality in the human mind is subsumed under Marxist cognitive theory which states that the literary artist must portray reality in its totality, not by copying or photographing external phenomena. Marxism not only rejects the copying of reality, but also the notion that the art form is totally independent of reality, an abstraction of reality. Hence, Lukacs' critique of Modernism as art alienated from social reality. Marxist cognitive theory, the theory of reflection, claims that modern abstract art does not express the dialectic between essence and phenomena. Dialectical thought perceives reality on various levels: the surface reality of flux, which does not recur; and more profound, essential tendencies which do recur. This dialectic pervades reality so that "phenomena" and "essence" are relativized; that which appeared to be essence when first discovered, will turn out to be a phenomenon behind which new essence is created. Literary art should reflect this process by which phenomena reveal themselves as essence through dynamic change.

Lukacs claims that literature has become fetichized, become exchangeable merchandise in the period of Modernism. Subjectivity has degenerated into specialization and has turned into a luxurious commodity which is marketable because of the "personal stamp" of the artist. The artist's position in society has become tragic-comic, identical with prostitution.

> In both cases, this degeneration of humanity has the same social foundation, i.e., the divorce from the totality of society, the fetish-like separateness of any given part of one's activity, and a passive acceptance of spontaneity, which turns into a stagnant "philosophy", and which necessarily produces separation and fragmentation. The vending machine mentioned by Max Weber also claims its rightful existence here, but with a difference: it is no longer sentences and decisions that it spews out after having swallowed the coin, but "profound experiences". The death dance around the rationale of the commodities market has become slightly more macabre in this connection. A supermarket for pure, spontaneous experiences has been created, a dime store for the "ultimate things", a sellout of the human personality at sharply reduced prices. (J.V.) [2]

Art, then, changes its relationship to contemporary culture; this change is promoted and effectuated by the dichotomy between narrow bourgeois class interests and the vital demands of the total human culture. The division of labor is internalized, and this internalization turns into the most tragic factor to affect the literary artist in Capitalist society. Middle class culture, which has become a reflection of the commutation of use-value into exchange-value, exemplifies a deflation of the human values of freedom and equality, their dehumanization and reification, and their subsequent deconstruction into conventional institutions. The immediate effect of the fetichism of commodities is the obfuscation of essence and ideality, and the Modernist writer, who is himself placed in bourgeois culture, is thus doubly alienated: he is estranged from his own class and also divorced from the cultural ideal itself, the manifestation and representation of the human spirit. His art must by necessity become an attempt to negate his own class; but by doing this, he succumbs, ironically, to the division of labor, because he becomes a specialist, marketing himself by prostituting his own "use-value" as a human subject, his private experience. The division of labor becomes not only the primary cause of cultural disintegration and the dissociation of sensibility; it also produces the introjection of dichotomies and divergencies, divergencies which manifest themselves as a dualistic approach to philosophical, psychological, and aesthetic problems. Dualistic systems of thought coincide with and express the economic and social problematic that is related to the division of labor, and an identical dualism becomes apparent in aesthetic form and content, as an ironic discrepancy between the essence of feeling and thought in its unified symbolic representation and the surface phenomena of social reality which are embedded in the literary work as structural fragmentation.

Revelation as symbolic representation, as a process of re-symbolization, takes the form of a dialectic between repressed material and utopian projection or image-making. The utopian is an expression of essence as actual, non-repressed reality and humanity, and the realistic genre in literature is, perhaps, the most adequate and complete manifestation of the culture. With the advent of Modernism, the utopian quality is further and further estranged due to the Capitalist mode of production, and Modernism is a deficient expression of the totality of life, according to Marxist aesthetics. In my opinion, however, the utopian impulse manifests itself in Modernism as the nuclear imagination which creates a private symbolic space designed to reconcile the dichotomy between human integration and societal fragmentation.

The division of labor also manifests itself in the dialectics of human perception, as we saw it in Lukacs' description of essence and phenomena and in Marx's explication of the fetichism of commodities. The dialectic of essence and phenomena finds its parallel and its symptomatic representation in Freud's meta-psychology and Kierkegaard's modes of consciousness to the extent, even, that we can speak of a direct structural identity between Marx's and Kierkegaard's theories of perception. Freud is a slightly different matter, of course, but his primary dualism, the one between the life and death instincts, can be interpreted as a psychological determinism rooted in the division of labor, the estrangement of "body" from "spirit" or "essence", where the phenomena, sexual and biological, of the body are relegated to a primordial darkness which manifests itself demonically as aggression and death in a kind of counterattack of the repressed bodily organism which has been divorced from its own structural principle, its own unified essence, spirit. Freud occupies a place similar to that of the modernist writer: he must explicate the system he is subservient to; he must represent it and at the same time distance himself from it by creating a "utopian" idea, that of Eros, to counteract the social divisions which become introjected in Freudian psychoanalysis, de-symbolized and transformed into intrapsychic phenomena and libidinal instincts which are distributed and separated among the mental agencies, id, ego, and super-ego.

In Kierkegaard's philosophy of perception, spirit plays a part identical to that of Freud's Eros and Marx's essence; the surface phenomena of social reality, which Marx discloses through material dialectics, and which conceal the human essence of history, correspond to sense data and sense impressions in Kierkegaard's analysis of human perception. Sense data are converted to general concepts or ideas; general ideas that are not converted to concrete subjective action through the transformational process of consciousness, remain in the sphere of static repetition, the objective sphere, to which aesthetics belongs as an objective science. The esthete's relationship to general ideas and concepts (<u>almenforestillinger</u>) is reflective, and objective reflection expresses itself as a disinterested relation to the objects of the world; Johannes' relationship to Cordelia does not create a dialectic between self and object, but an obliteration or preclusion of self and of subjective interest which prevents suffering, despair, and pathos, but which also excludes the esthete from the creation of a subjective mode of consciousness which is a prerequisite for action in the real world and for continuity in life. Mere reflection is on the abstract level of pure logic, and Kierkegaard's critique of Hegelian thought is based on this insight. The dimension which Kierkegaard adds to the concept of historical dialectics is the one of subjective consciousness, which he interprets as the mediator between ideality and reality, between body and soul, and between the timely and the eternal, with the moment, øjeblikket, functioning as the infusion of dialectical movement into the individual consciousness. Consciousness and history thus become, they are the becoming, det tilblivende, and static repetition of general ideas (which Kierkegaard calls "recollection" in the "Greek sense") becomes, through its integration with becoming reality, transformed into dynamic recurrence, repetition of spirit in motion, gentagelse. Kierkegaard emphasizes that the individual realizes himself through the commutation of consciousness that takes place in the transition from the aesthetical to the ethical stage; the latter is reflection on self and concretization of the subject in its relation to the real social world; the ethical ideal is realized in individual activity, a process which, for Marx too, is instigated by the subjective transformation of history through the activity of human labor. There is thus some identity between Marx's and Kierkegaard's formulations of dialectical thought and the progress of history; that which Marx calls "false consciousness", i.e., the transformation of use-value to exchange-value and the subsequent reification of human and social relationships, corresponds to Kierkegaard's aesthetic mode of life, where thought is based on sense data and general ideas, and where intellect manifests itself as the static relation between the reflecting mind and its object; this is the primary reason why Johannes does not develop a kinetic love relationship to Cordelia in <u>Diary of a Seducer</u>.

By contrast, consciousness as consciousness of self, <u>interested</u> consciousness, is the dialectical locus of <u>inter-esse</u>, the "being-between", ideality and reality, which serves as the primary mover of the individual's concretion in history and time, i.e., the interested, serious fulfillment of the ethical ideal, its repletion with spirit, <u>aand</u>. Spirit, as the goal and fulfillment of consciousness, is itself identified as the kinetic dialectic of ideality and reality; whereas the bourgeois, conventional moral code is identified as the ethical ideal deprived of spirit and seriousness, the ideal deteriorated into a static, fixed idea, almenforestil-ling. An important integral part of dialectical consciousness is doubt, the essential form of which is inquiring doubt, i.e., the kind of doubt which critically enquires into the nature of sense data and general concepts in order to relate them to individual, psychological existence, to realize them in the concrete.

There are various internal and external obstacles to the evolution of reflection into doubt and self-consciousness; one psychological obstacle is what Freud has referred to as the compulsion to repeat, i.e., the tendency which, in the aesthetical mode of life, manifests itself as objective reflection, reflection without emotional content. I must emphasize that I view the esthete's "compulsion to repeat", his quantifying of existence, as a preliminary expression of the mythopoetic consciousness that mirrors general concepts which later evolve into the "transcendental", or into "essence" in Marxist terms. The mythopoetic nature of the esthete contains, in modern terms, the negation of fixed compulsions, i.e, the nuclear imagination which will, through the consciousness of dialectical time, project itself as resymbolization, as a concrete second reality, a superimposition of real human integration upon the fragmented, dualistic reality which our senses perceive. The obscure nature of social reality and the obfuscation of human spirit assume equally important positions in Kierkegaard's, Freud's and Marx's philosophical thought, and this fact indicates that their philosophies are the "signs" of fundamentally identical historical problems, problems which extend into Modernity and literary Modernism itself. For the purpose of a dialectical exposition, a clarification of structural and developmental parallels, I have chosen to abstract somewhat from Kierkegaard's, Marx's and Freud's contemporary intellectual contexts; I want to re-think their respective systems as they relate to the modern era, as they create a "futuristic" dialectic, so to speak. This abstraction, however, is no distortion of their ideologies, merely testimony to the fact that these ideologies are indeed applicable to the modern period because of the socioeconomic, historical, and ontological bases common to 19th century individualism and 20th century individualism, i.e., the common emphasis on the subjective, which Lukacs incorrectly describes as an abstract subjectivity; it is concrete subjectivity which I interpret as the revolt of the subject against objective de-humanization and alienation.

The internal estrangement from spirit, which is a preoccupation with Kierkegaard, is fundamentally related to Freud's metapsychological dualism and to Marx's concept of alienation and fetichism, the objectivation or reification of personal relationships. The relationship between Johannes and Cordelia represents a reified emotive behavior, in that the reflective thought process of the Seducer is divorced from emotional, interested content; and Kierkegaard's demonic category represents the extremest point of emotional and societal alienation, as it reflects the inversion, or exacerbation of the philistine moral code, an institutionalized "fear of the good". The demonic marks the deterioration of the ideal into emptiness and into a codified pattern of repetition which excludes recurrence (of spirit) and continuity (of history), gentagelse and det tilblivende. The exclusion of the demonic from its participation in history reveals the socioeconomic aspect of the demonic, its manifestation as a Marxian social type epitomizing human estrangement. The demonic, and to a lesser extent the esthete, is also a psychological type who is disposed, by internal compulsion and by external, socioeconomic necessity, to live outside the human dimension and the historical totality.

I indicated earlier that the demonic category also represents a re-sexualization of the Oedipal conflict; I can now interpret this re-sexualization as an impotent rebellion against the "sadistic" superego, the oppressive upper class which has institutionalized the "good" and inculcated it into individual middle class consciousness where it functions as a regulator and controller of the libido and as a de-politicizing agency. The demonic type, as a social outcast, performs a rebellion which is, ironically, a form of subservience, masochism; the demonic person mistakes conventional "good" for ethical ideal, and confuses actual freedom with false consciousness, although the knowledge and perception of freedom is inherent in, as well as external to, the demonic. As Kierkegaard puts it, freedom comes to it "from the outside", forcing the demonic to reveal and express itself; but the demonic expresses itself against its own will, and through de-symbolization, i.e., meaningless language. The demonic is therefore the ideal transmuted into emptiness, symbolic meaning deprived of linguistic sense and coherence. The "masochism" of the demonic becomes, in socioeconomic terms, a repressed, silent form of "putting up with" the state of de-humanization, alienation, and with the reification of human relationships.

This kind of "re-thinking" of Kierkegaard's demonic category makes it clear that Freud also has to be re-thought, because of the fundamental re-structuring of the Oedipal situation that occurs in post-industrial Capitalism. The most important aspect of this re-structuring is the absence or disappearance of the father figure, which means that the object of the subject's rebellion is no longer clearly delineated; consequently, the individual finds it difficult to realize himself, to become individuated; this difficulty is identical to the obscurity and complexity of Kierkegaard's demonic category - the demonic is the product of a psychological fixation and of a defective cognitive process which dimly recognizes freedom, but which does not fully understand the free dimension of existence. Freedom was created, in part, through a revolt against the despotic father, in earlier periods. Kierkegaard, already, prevised the post-industrial society when he described the demonic category and its complex "shut-upness", for this shut-upness is false consciousness, the introjected and extrajected obscurity which is created by alienation from human essence and by the neutralization of social class conflicts.

The re-structuring of the Oedipal situation forces the individual to seek new forms of self-expression and identity; Herbert Marcuse's re-thinking of Freud is formulated as a description of the absent father figure in modern society, and the substitution of the "maternal super-id" for the father image.

> One more step in the interpretation, and the strange traces of the "superid" appear as traces of a different, lost reality, or lost relation between ego and reality. The notion of reality which is predominant in Freud and which is condensed in the reality principle is "bound up with the father." It confronts the id and the ego as a hostile, external force, and, accordingly, the father is chiefly a hostile figure, whose power is symbolized in the castration-threat, "directed against the gratification of libidinal urges toward the mother." The growing ego attains maturity by complying with this hostile force: "submission to the castration threat" is the "decisive step in the establishment of the ego as based on the reality principle." However, this reality which the ego faces as an outside antagonistic power is neither the only nor the primary reality. The development of the ego is development "away from primary narcissism"; at this early stage, reality "is not outside, but is contained in the pre-ego of primary narcissism." It is not hostile and alien to the ego, but "intimately connected with, originally not even distinguished from it." This reality is first (and last?) experienced in the child's libidinal relation to the mother - a relation which is at the beginning within the "pre-ego" and only subsequently divorced from it. And with this division of the original unity, an "urge towards re-establishing the original unity" develops: a "libidinal flow between

infant and mother." At this primary stage
of the relation between "pre-ego" and
reality, the Narcissistic and the maternal
Eros seem to be one, and the primary experience
of reality is that of a libidinous union.
The Narcissistic phase of individual pre-
genitality "recalls" the maternal phase of
the history of the human race. Both con-
stitute a reality to which the ego responds
with an attitude, not of defense and submission, but of integral identification with
the "environment." But in the light of
the paternal reality principle, the "maternal concept" of reality here emerging is
immediately turned into something negative,
dreadful. The impulse to re-establish the
lost Narcissistic-maternal unity is interpreted as a "threat," namely, the threat of
"maternal engulfment" by the overpowering
womb. The hostile father is exonerated and
reappears as savior who, in punishing the
incest wish, protects the ego from its anni-
hilation in the mother. The question does
not arise whether the Narcissistic-maternal
attitude toward reality cannot "return" in
less primordial, less devouring forms under
the power of the mature ego and in a mature
civilization. Instead, the necessity of
suppressing this attitude once and for all
is taken for granted. The patriarchal reality
principle holds sway over the psychoanalytic
interpretation. It is only beyond this
reality principle that the "maternal" images
of the super ego convey promises rather than
memory traces - images of a free future
rather than of a dark past.[3]

The disappearance of the authoritarian father, i.e.
of oppression within the cellular family unit, evokes a
potential re-integration of Death and Eros in a mature
civilization; but the intermediary stage between the
original Oedipus complex and the dissolution of this

complex poses problems. The superego is greatly weakened, so that the newly liberated individual is denied the path to self-realization and emancipation once offered him by the revolt against the father:

> On the political level, the withdrawal of the right to revolt against the father is reproduced as a disappearance of any effective possibility of negating the system in general. The weakening of the class struggle, the assimilation of the working classes into the bourgeoisie, is the objective condition for this universal neutralization; and with the extension of the media, the very content and gestures of revolt are exhausted, in the sense in which television performers speak of the "exhaustion" of their raw material through over-exposure. In this sense, tolerance in our society can be said to be genuinely repressive, in that it offers a means of defusing the most dangerous and subversive ideas: not censorship, but the transformation into a fad, is the most effective way of destroying a potentially threatening movement or revolutionary personality.[4]

The task of the philosopher and the literary artist, under these circumstances, is to revive the idea of the *negative*, which Marcuse formulates as the revival of the utopian impulse, the imaginative reconstruction of a political hermeneutic, which Jameson describes as follows:

> For hermeneutics, traditionally a technique whereby religions recuperated the texts and spiritual activities of cultures resistant to them, is also a political discipline, and provides the means for maintaining contact with the very

sources of revolutionary energy during a stagnant time, of preserving the concept of freedom itself, underground, during geological ages of repression. Indeed, it is the concept of freedom which, measured against those other possible ones of love of justice, happiness or work, proves to be the privileged instrument of a political hermeneutic, and which, in turn, is perhaps itself best understood as an interpretive device rather than a philosophical essence or idea. For wherever the concept of freedom is once more understood, it always comes as the awakening of dissatisfaction in the midst of all that is — at one, in that, with the birth of the negative itself: never a state that is enjoyed, or a mental structure that is contemplated, but rather an ontological impatience in which the constraining situation itself is for the first time perceived in the very moment in which it is refused. From the physical intimidation of the Fascist state to the agonizing repetitions of neurosis, the idea of freedom takes the same temporal form: a sudden perception of an intolerable present which is at the same time, but implicitly and however dimly articulated, the glimpse of another state in the name of which the first is judged. Thus the idea of freedom involves a kind of perceptual superposition; it is a way of reading the present, but it is a reading that looks more like the reconstruction of an extinct language.

This formal character of the concept of freedom is precisely what lends itself to the work of political hermeneutics. It encourages analogy: assimilating the material prisons to the psychic ones, it serves as a means of unifying all these separate levels of existence, functioning, indeed, as a kind of transformational equation whereby the data characteristic of one may be converted into the terms of other. It is not too much to say that the concept of freedom thus permits us to transcend one of the most fundamental contradictions in modern existence: that between the outside and the inside, between public and private, work and leisure, the sociological and the psychological, between my being-for-others and my being-for-myself, between the

political and the poetic, objectivity and
subjectivity, the collective and the solitary -
between society and the monad. It is an
opposition which the confrontation between
Marx and Freud dramatizes emblematically; and
the persistence of this attempted confrontation
(Reich, the Surrealists, Sartre, left-wing
Structuralism, not to speak of Marcuse himself)
underlines the urgency with which modern man
seeks to overcome his double life, his dis-
persed and fragmentary existence.[5]

The utopian idea, which is the projection of freedom and of a second reality, is the negation of the here and now, which occurs as a product of hermeneutical analysis, i.e., deciphering of the obscurities and illusions inherent in post-industrial Capitalism, a deciphering which is a re-interpretation of Marx and Freud, a bringing them up to date. The utopian idea is the impulse of fantasy in which alone the Freudian pleasure principle is liberated and recollected. The memory of a unified, integrated existence which, for Marcuse, manifests itself in the culture as the "maternal super-id", is the kinetic re-absorption into consciousness of creative motion, of Kierkegaard's becoming, <u>det tilblivende</u>. Future time and history is thus created as a dialectical synthesizing of internal impulses and historical models, and "utopia" is the actualization of self brought about by the creative imagination, by the process of resymbolization. The utopian idea is equivalent to the Marxian idea of essence, human totality as it is unfolded underneath the fragmented surface of things. It is also equivalent to Kierkegaard's spirit, which is the re-integration of body and soul, the timely and the eternal.

Both Kierkegaard's, Marx's, and Freud's philosophies can, therefore, be regarded as hermeneutical systems designed to interpret human psychology, ethics, and society; they can also be seen as hermeneutical projections of an ideological reintegration in the creative imagination, and for this reason I view the poetic or mythic constructs of Kierkegaard's esthete as the hermetic veils of a transcendental revelation, which is to occur during the transformational process of human consciousness. The transformation of memory, <u>erindring</u>, to recurrence, <u>gentagelse</u>, is an evolution of consciousness which points to the hermeneutical aspect of Modernism, i.e., the process whereby subjective material is lifted to awareness of itself, resymbolized, and re-integrated literarily and ideologically.

I see Knut Hamsun's novel <u>Hunger</u> as a literary attempt to re-establish the lost Narcissistic-maternal unity by employing the utopian impulse, i.e., by creating an imaginary, symbolic space which reconciles and reintegrates the poles of the primary dissonance between private subject and social object. The novel illustrates the Modernistic dissonance on three levels: 1) dissonance between private subject and poetic subject (manipulating author); 2) dissonance between the poeticized subject and the social space; 3) dissonance between the objective social conditions which embody the neutralization and the de-personalization of the human subject through false consciousness, reification, and alienation, <u>and</u> the imaginary symbolic space which recreates a primary unity between the self and the real world as it is projected into what Marcuse calls the "negative", i.e., a second reality which is emancipated from its suppressed state of being in the world of surface phenomena.

The ironic contrast between the conditions of literary art and the response of the artist to those conditions is inserted into <u>Hunger</u> as a formalistic principle which manifests itself as a divergence, consciously contrived, between emotive behavior and reflective analysis; this principle works at the most local level of the novel, in the individual paragraph. The protagonist acts and comments on his own actions at the same time. I see this as the hermeneutical process at work in its most basic and minute form, namely the attachment of impulsive emotions to a partly obscure reality and the simultaneous liberation of poetic images and symbols through consciousness; this is a deciphering process through which literary description and presentation of the Modernist condition transcends that condition; it is the self-transcendence of Modernism.

This dual function of writing and being conscious of the writing process manifests itself as an evocation of demonic fixation, the primordial darkness of the body, coupled with aesthetic and lyrical liberation and resolution, which leads to a synthesizing of the body-soul dualism through the recurrence of lyrical and symbolic imagery in the novel. <u>Hunger</u> is the creative process by which the objective social condition and its concurrent, demonically fixated private imagery is sublimated and liberated through the literary form, and through the act of writing. The re-sexualization of the demonic, which I saw as reflective of a passive submission to philistine conventions, a "masochistic" fear of the good, evolves into an active, integrated sexuality which strives to become re-united with the female, the maternal, as the life-giving cultural matrix. In this novel, I see the possibility of a dynamic re-absorption of the demonic into the growing, developing personality. This evolution presupposes a cognition of the cultural fragmentation caused, partly, by the division of labor, which the artist must overcome by seeing through it and writing through it. By the creative process itself, the state of primordial darkness into which the body has been cast due to the specialization (under Capitalism) of the poet as "salesman of spiritual experiences" is integrated with light, spirit. The poet who has been split off from his own physical self that is the object of his hunger, reconciles physical and intellectual self through creative activity. The frozen traits and gestures of the divided personality that interacts with itself in a static, mechanical manner, are dissolved by the dynamics of literary form, which operates on the "utopian" impulse, i.e., the impulse to re-unite with the maternal Eros.

The protagonist describes his own self-conscious writing process:

> For several minutes the work went on swiftly. Speech after speech popped up in my head perfectly formed and I wrote on without a pause. I filled one sheet after the other, leaped over all obstacles, humming softly in delight over my rich mood. I was almost unconscious of myself. The only sound I heard during all this time was my own joyful humming. I got a new idea too, an excellent one, about a church bell that would suddenly burst out ringing at a certain point in the plot. Everything went marvelously.

> Then I heard steps on the stairs. I shivered and almost leaped out of my skin; at that moment I was timorous, wary, afraid of everything, oversensitive from hunger. I listened nervously, held my hand and the pencil motionless, and listened - I couldn't write a single word. The door opened, the pair from the living room walked in. 6

At the moment of writing, he is perched on a chair by the door - he no longer has his own room - and his body is curved, forming an external shell around the private space of his consciousness; the division of labor has become internalized: the poet is private, but his privacy is invaded, he must exhibit himself to the public; the scene epitomizes the public exhibition of the poet, and his reliance on the public for material and commercial support. The hero's writings are, for the most part, designed to be articles for commercial consumption; he writes about any subject on earth in order to get money to live on. This objective material condition is reflected in literary creation and perception as an attachment to fleeting, discontinuous sense impressions from the street, and it is reflected in the temporal structure of the novel as a lack of continuity, history, and identity.

> It was nine. The rattle of wagons and the hum of voices filled the air - growing into a great orchestra of sound into which the noise of people walking

> and the cracks of the drivers' whips fit perfectly. The traffic noise on all sides cheered me up immediately, and I began to feel more content and at peace. I had much more to do of course than merely to take a morning stroll in the fresh air. What did my lungs care for fresh air? I was powerful as a giant and could stop a wagon with my shoulders. A rare and delicate mood, a feeling of wonderful light-heartedness had taken hold of me. I began examining the people I met or passed, I read the posters on walls, noticed a glance thrown at me from a streetcar, let every trivial occurrence influence me, every tiny detail that crossed my eyes and vanished. 7

His state of "light carelessness" is enforced by his physical hunger, which turns into a productive state of mind, the most extreme manifestation of the self-division by which the narrator-protagonist "feeds" on his own body, makes it hypersensitive to external stimuli by starving it.

> Thoughts of God began to occupy me again. It seemed to me utterly reprehensible of Him to block my way every time I tried for a job and to ruin my chances when it was only daily bread that I was asking for. I had noticed very clearly that every time I went hungry a little too long it was as though my brains simply ran quietly out of my head and left me empty. My head became light and floating, I could no longer feel its weight on my shoulders, and I had the sense that my eyes were remaining far too open when I looked at anything. 8

Awareness of the body as the emblem of a continuous personal history, an identity, is actually analyzed by

the hero as weakness, a defect which will spoil his
poetic vision:

> In this instant, my head was so clear that I could
> follow the most difficult train of thought without
> any effort. Lying in this position, letting my
> eyes float down over my chest and legs, I noticed
> the tiny leaping movement my feet made every time
> my heart beat. I sat up partway and gazed down
> at my feet. At that moment a strange and fantastic
> mood came over me which I had never felt before -
> a delicate and wonderful shock ran through all
> of my nerves as though a stream of light had
> flowed through them. As I stared at my shoes, I
> felt as if I had met an old friend, or got back
> some part of me that had been torn off: a feeling
> of recognition went through me, tears came to my
> eyes, and I experienced my shoes as a soft whispering
> sound coming up toward me. "Getting weak!" I said
> fiercely to myself and I closed my fists and said,
> "Getting weak." I was furious with myself for
> these ridiculous sensations, which had overpowered
> me even though I was fully conscious of them.
> I spoke harsh and sensible phrases, and I closed
> my eyes tightly to get rid of the tears. Then
> I began, as though I had never seen my shoes
> before, to study their expression, their shape,
> and the worn-out leather they had; and I dis-
> covered that their wrinkles and their white seams
> gave them an expression, provided them with a
> face. Something of my own being had gone over
> into these shoes, they struck me as being a ghost
> of my "I", a breathing part of myself 9

At this point, he sees his body, and his foot, as
a breathing part of himself, a potentially integrated
sensory apparatus without which he cannot be whole.
He gives up the wholeness, however, in order to produce,

and succumbs temporarily to the demands of the objective social condition.

> Delusions and dreams! I told myself that if I did eat food now, my head would get upset again, I would have the same feverish brain and ridiculous ideas to deal with. I simply couldn't take food; I wasn't made that way; that was one of my characteristics, a peculiar thing with me. 10

The hero is accurate in his description of his revulsion for food as a peculiarity: it is his special feature, <u>qua</u> poet, to be a highly sensitized barometer of reality, and his sensitivity becomes marketable through its exclusiveness; it is his exchange-value, his poetry as commodity, and he depends entirely on the newspaper editor for money, and subsequently on the consuming "literary" public. The darkness into which the body is cast becomes the birthplace of a poetically esoteric language, a sub-literary language; a deformed, meaningless word is created, a word which can mean anything, <u>kuboå</u>.

> I still was not sleepy, however, and could not fall asleep. I remained a while looking into the dark - this dense substance of darkness that had no bottom, which I couldn't understand. My thoughts could not grasp such a thing. It seemed to be dark beyond all measurement, and I felt its presence weigh me down. I closed my eyes and took to singing half aloud and rocking myself back and forth on the cot to amuse myself, but it did no good. The dark had

> captured my brain and gave me not an instant of
> peace. What if I myself become dissolved into the
> dark, turned into it? I sat up in bed and struck
> out with my arms.
> My nervous condition had completely taken over,
> and no amount of struggle against it helped. I sat
> there, a prey to the weirdest fantasies, gurgling
> to myself, humming lullabies, sweating in my effort
> to be calm. I stared out into the dark, and had
> never in all my life seen such blackness. There
> was no doubt that what I was faced with here was
> a special kind of blackness, an extreme element
> which no one before had ever noticed. The most
> ridiculous ideas occupied me, and everything
> frightened me. 11

The word promotes a fantasy of death and darkness by which the poet travels to sea on board the "black monsters", the ships in the harbor. The darkness through which he is propelled is his own non-ego, his unsubstantial self which is invaded by a mass of dark space and filled with it.

> I opened my eyes. How could I keep them closed
> when I couldn't sleep! The same darkness was
> brooding around me, the same fathomless black
> eternity which my intelligence fought against and
> could not grasp. What could I compare it to? I
> made the wildest, most desperate efforts to find
> a word black enough to suit that darkness, a word
> so hideously black that it would blacken my
> mouth when I said it. God in heaven, how black
> it was! And I started again to think about the
> harbor, the ships, the dark monsters who lay
> waiting for me. They wanted to pull me to them-
> selves and hold me fast and sail with me over
> land and sea, through dark kingdoms no man had
> ever seen. I felt myself on board ship, drawn on
> through waters, floating in clouds, going down,

> down .... I gave a hoarse shriek of fear, and
> hugged the bed; I had been on such a perilous
> journey, fallen down through the sky like a
> shot. How good and saved I felt when I grabbed the
> hard sides of the cot! That is what it is like to
> die, I said to myself, now I will die! 12

Co-existing with the realm of darkness is a realm of all-consuming fire, a conflagration of brains and books, sky and earth.

> Suddenly I remembered Ylayali. To think that I
> had forgotten her all night! Some light penetrated
> very weakly into my consciousness again, a tiny ray
> of sunlight, making me ecstatically warm. More sun-
> light flowed in, a gentle delicate silky light,
> which brushed so sweetly against me. Then the
> sun grew stronger and stronger, blazing brilliantly
> on my temples, piercing with heavy and burning heat
> into my emaciated brain. At the end a mad open fire
> blazed up before my eyes, a heaven and an earth
> ignited, men and animals of fire, mountains of fire,
> devils of fire, a chaos, a wilderness, a universe
> on fire, a smoking final day. 13

The darkness, however, has positive connotations, too; it has a light and a music of its own:

> The darkness brooded around me. Nothing moved. But
> high above my head rustled endless music, the air,
> that distant tuneless humming which never fell
> silent. I listened so long to this eternal feeble
> sound that it began to get me confused: it was
> certainly symphonies coming from the orbiting
> universes above me, stars that were singing a
> song 14

The dark monsters do not only conduct him to destruction, and are not exclusively symbolic of the abnegation of the body as identity and erotic vehicle; they also have a cathartic purpose: they destroy one self in order to gain another self. The stars that "intone a song" are the primary natural symbols which evoke an incipient re-integration, in the private symbolic space, of the light-darkness paradox and the private-public dichotomy which the artist is forced to endure as an objective social condition. The use of nature symbolism becomes the first tentative attempt to recreate the natural unity of body and spirit. The hero's poetic imagination does not dissociate itself from the organic social totality, but tries to recapture it through recollection.

In the novel as a whole, two separate forms and functions of recollection can be distinguished, namely the mnemonics of the temporal structure whose function it is to <u>isolate</u> sense data, not unite them into organic units. Mnemonics is the form and function of literary fragmentation, and manifests itself, for example, as the hero's unawareness of time and place; the mnemonics consists of fragmented sense impressions, which, ironically, are essential to the protagonist because he survives financially (not too well!) by selling them. On the marketplace which represents deflated, dissociated values, moral chaos, cultural fragmentation, and the quantifying of substance that is conducive to reification, the poet's "intense", "private" experience is commercialized and promoted to exchange-value.

The poet's perception and cognition of this circumstance produces a creative reaction by which he transforms the body-spirit paradox into a mutuality of Death and Eros, their reintegration. At the level of recurrent symbolic imagery and symbolic experience, a real recurrence takes place, a substantial recollection of personal unity and continuity, the Kierkegaardian gentagelse, which is the commutation of memory and sense data into identity. The formation of subjective value is a continuous undercurrent in Hunger; it shapes the artist's response to his own paradoxical situation, his "tragic-comic" position in society, as Lukacs puts it. The objective social condition to which the hunger-hero reacts has, in a sense, produced the optimal vantage point for artistic creativity: for the social condition, as it is internalized, injects a recognition of its own opposite, its own negative, into the artist. I must point out, however, that the social conditions remain traumatic and detrimental almost throughout the novel, and the hero's most significant literary experiment is a play about a prostitute who is consumed by flames, and the artist compares himself to the prostitute, another dealer in "private" merchandise.

But it is clear that there is a progressive, dynamic change in the imagery surrounding darkness in the novel. That imagery had been at its lowest point in the prison cell where the hero's lack of a sense of his own body, his lack of identity made him experience the invasion of a frightening, primordial darkness through which he plunged in a death-like fall, unable to reach his own body, unable to let go, experiencing, perhaps, failure to achieve orgasm. This darkness is transposed into the element of light, where the re-integration of Death and Eros is accomplished as a recurrence of a primary experience, the fusion of the poet with his dream woman, Ylajali:

> Not a sound came to disturb me - the soft dark had hidden the whole world from me, and buried me in a wonderful peace - only the desolate voice of stillness sounded monotonously in my ear. And the dark monsters out there wanted to pull me to themselves as soon as night came, and they wanted to take me far far over seas and through strange lands where no human being lives. And they wanted to bring me to Princess Ylayali's castle, where an undreamed-of happiness was waiting for me, greater than any

person's! And she herself would be sitting in a
blazing room all of whose walls were amethyst, on a
throne of yellow roses, and she would reach her
hands out to me when I entered, greet me, and cry
"Welcome" as I came near to her and kneeled: "Welcome,
O knight, to me and my land! I have been waiting twenty summers for you, and have called your name every
bright summer night, and when you were in grief I
wept here, and when you slept I breathed marvelous
dreams into your head ...." And the beautiful creature took my hand as I rose, and led me on through
long corridors where huge crowds of people shouted
Hurrah, through sunlit orchards where three hundred
young girls were playing and laughing, and into another chamber made all of brilliant emerald. The sun
shone into it, choral music floated through galleries
and halls toward me, perfumed air moved over me. I
held her hand in mine, and felt a mad occult delight
shoot through my blood; I put my arms around her and
she whispered:" Not here, come farther in!" So we
walked into the red chamber all of whose walls were
ruby - an overwhelming joy which made me faint. Then
I felt her arms around me, she breathed in my face,
whispering:" Welcome now, my sweet! Kiss me! Again ....
again ...."
  From my bench I saw stars in front of my eyes and
my thought shot forward into a tornado of light 15

The passage emphasizes the identity between the hero and the woman, and unequivocally points to the experience as a recalled and relived one. She has been waiting for him for twenty summers and has called to him during nights of light, and she has breathed dreams into him.

In the "real" social space, then, the body-spirit dichotomy remains fixed as an outcome of the division of labor; in the private symbolic space, the conflagration and death of the body is sublimated through a cathartic experience, and transformed into Ylajali's erotic light, which signals the trans-substantiation of social reality into the negative, the subjective negation that occurs within the private utopian space. In this symbolic space, I see a potentially revolutionary social critique; the private negative is the prerequisite for a reformed social reality. The division of labor is abolished in the symbolic dream space which signifies that an ideological reconcilation has occurred, and that the poet is re-united with the cultural matrix. The hero's idea of freedom has been produced by a perceptual superposition: linguistic and poetic reconstruction, recurrence of an extinct identity.

CHAPTER III REFERENCES

[1] Karl Marx, <u>Capital</u>, Volume I. (New York: International Publishers, 1967), p. 72.

[2] Georg Lukacs, <u>Kunst og kapitalisme</u>. (København: Nordisk Forlag, 1971), p. 96.

[3] Herbert Marcuse, <u>Eros and Civilization</u>. (Boston: The Beacon Press, 1974), pp. 229-231.

[4] Fredric Jameson, <u>Marxism and Form</u>. (Princeton, New Jersey: Princeton University Press, 1971), p. 110.

[5] Jameson, pp. 84-85.

[6] Knut Hamsun, <u>Hunger</u>, trans. Robert Bly (New York: Farrar, Straus and Giroux, 1967), pp. 218-219.

[7] Hamsun, pp. 6-7.

[8] Hamsun, p. 21.

[9] Hamsun, pp. 23-24.

[10] Hamsun, p. 46

[11] Hamsun, pp. 76-77.

[12] Hamsun, p. 80.

[13] Hamsun, p. 157.

[14]Hamsun, p. 49.

[15]Hamsun, pp. 69-70.

CHAPTER 4

THE AESTHETICS OF REPETITION.
A PORTRAIT, ULYSSES, HAVOC.

In *Diary of a Seducer*, Søren Kierkegaard described the male-female dualism, sexual difference, as an outcome of Johannes' reductive vision, his limited perception of the nature of femininity. Johannes' ideology divided woman (nature) from man (thought), thus producing a psychological and existential estrangement from spirit. This estrangement was, in Freudian terms, the product of a failure to integrate subject and object sexually, i.e., unequal distribution of libido. Cordelia could be seen as Johannes' own "nature", a projection of his own sexuality on to the female, i.e., object-cathexis. This object-cathexis produced reflection and sexual consciousness in Cordelia, and she was seen to approach the state of integrated spirit, or, the re-union of body and soul, nature and thought, into a higher synthesis.

In Marxist terms, the male-female separation, and the internal division between thought and nature that operates in Johannes as incomplete cognition of the totality of reality, occurs as a product of the division of labor which turned Johannes into a "specialist", a seducer, who controls reality and other people by maintaining distance and by projecting a lack of emotional interest, although this lack of interest produces a significant change in the "other", the female, pointing to Johannes' fulfilling the "specializing" function of mediator, in an aesthetic sense. His artful deceit does not express self-interest, but causes female interest to come about, in that it poses the mediating link between thought and nature, the inter-esse.

The Seducer's Don Juan-like quantification of existence could be interpreted as an obfuscation of actual social and personal relationships, a falsification of human "use-value" and its subsequent transformation into "exchange-value", i.e., the equalization of all value. The Seducer attempts, instinctively and consciously, to prevent or reduce the equalization of value by creating myth and poetry; this activity elevates female nature into poetic principle and poetic muse, and in my discussion of Diary of a Seducer, I saw this creative process as a possible liberation from and neutralization of the male-female dualism, an internalization and reabsorption of the female as a culturally and socially generative matrix; the aesthetic stage means, then, an at least partial subjectivizing of the objective, the "other", and can, therefore, be seen as a potential

<u>longing</u> for the transcendental, the subjective, religious absolute which forms Kierkegaard's final existential mode. This reading of Kierkegaard creates, basically, a re-thinking of Kierkegaard, by which I place him within the social context of 19th century middle class society, and at the same time, lift him out of that context by examining the dialectical relationship between the Danish philosopher and 20th century Modernism. The division between male and female is, ultimately, a socioeconomic division and must be seen as a separation of social and sexual roles that is due to the divided interests and role functions of 19th century class society; and Kierkegaard's (and Johannes') internalization of female nature and sexuality and their subsequent conversion into fuel for the creative process makes him a Modernist with a singular <u>will to art</u>.

Class divisions were exacerbated further in the late 19th century, as we saw it in Hamsun's <u>Hunger</u>, where the artist is totally alienated from his class and from his own body. The process of emancipation from class divisions takes on a more painful form, as these divisions are further internalized and loaded with emotive content. The class separation is, however, transcended

in <u>Hunger</u> as the artist becomes re-integrated with the
cultural matrix through the creative function of dream.
Preceding this re-integration, the artist lived through
a cathartic experience of death, an experience which
meant the obliteration of personal history and identity
as a prerequisite for re-uniting with the "id", or "it",
the sexually undifferentiated, androgynous psyche, which
is, paradoxically, a highly erotic and almost religious
reunion of male and female, of poet and cultural matrix.
The re-unification of poet and cultural matrix is not
only a transcendence of class divisions, but also a
transcendence of the neutralization and pacification
of the class conflict which occur in later, post-
industrial Capitalism. The androgynous union of the
hunger-hero and Ilajali is a pre-Oedipal, narcissistic
union in a positive sense, a Marcusian "negative", which
reaffirms subjective value; the reunion also creates a
re-integration of individual and type, of the particular
and the universal, a re-integration which Lukacs claims
is not extant in Modernism. Modernism, from my point
of view, is highly political, in that it visualizes, by
poetic symbol and metaphor, a re-integrated, mature individual who, in a sense, is the Communist type Lukacs
is looking for high and low in Modernism, at least if

we see Communism as the equal and free interaction between fully mature, integrated individuals. The equal distribution of sexual libido and psychic energy throughout the body (male-female body) is, in a sense, the equivalence of the equal distribution of capital and freedom in a mature society, and the emblem of this society, its "type", is the androgynous individual. The "super-id" of the cultural matrix is, then, the psychological and sociological foundation for individual and political liberation.

The liberation process in Hunger was also interpreted as a dialectical integration of memory and recurrence, Kierkegaard's gentagelse. The memory and sense data of past and present were lifted out of the context of flux, fragmentation and discontinuity through hermeneutic resymbolization, i.e., the re-attachment of meaning to a private universe that had become increasingly detached from social reality, a reality that was in itself progressively fragmented; the reunion of private individual and social type, therefore, had to occur within a symbolic space that re-integrated individually and socially fragmented reality through an unconscious and conscious projection of an extinct identity. This complex process of emancipation is seen, of course, as a subjective transcendence of the social condition that made it almost impossible for the artist to create his art and to induce that art into the sphere of public communication - where it rightly belongs - since the communication process itself had become reified and commercialized.

The duality of "memory" and "recurrence" is conceptualized by Kierkegaard's pseudonym Constantin Constantius in Repetition:

> Repetition and memory are the same processes, but move in opposite directions; for what is remembered, what has been, is repeated backwards; whereas actual repetition is recalled forward. Therefore, if repetition is at all possible, it will make a person happy, while recollection will make him unhappy, assuming that he takes the time to live, and that he does not sneak away from life as soon as he is born on the pretext, for example, that he has forgotten something. (J.V.) 1

"Memory" is "remembering backwards", "recurrence" is "remembering forward". Repetition is continuity, becoming, and without it life is dissolved into "empty noise".

> The dialectic of repetition is easy; for what is repeated, has been, otherwise it could not be repeated, but the very fact that it has been makes the repetition of it into something new. When the Greeks said that all cognition is recollection, what they actually meant was that all of existence, which is, also has been; when one says that life

> is repetition, one intends to say: existence, which has been, is coming into being now. When one does not employ the category of recollection or repetition, then all of existence is dissolved into empty, meaningless noise. Recollection is the ethical view of life, repetition the modern one; repetition is the <u>interest</u> of metaphysics, and at the same time the <u>interest</u> upon which metaphysics is stranded; repetition is the password of any ethical viewpoint, and repetition is the <u>conditio</u> <u>sine</u> <u>qua</u> <u>non</u> for any dogmatic problem. (J.V.) 2

Memory that is unintegrated with recurrence can become a form of poetic existence, as represented by the young hero in Kierkegaard's philosophical novel. The female object of his reflection inspires longing, not love, and his longing induces poetic productivity.

> During the next two weeks, he visited me occasionally at my apartment. He was beginning to be aware of the mistake - the young girl he adored was becoming troublesome already. And yet she was his loved one, the only one he had loved, the only one he would ever love. On the other hand, he did not really love her; for he just longed for her. During all of this he went through a strange transformation. A poetic creativity awakened in him to an extent I had never thought possible. Now I saw everything clearly. The young girl was not his loved one; she merely brought on his creativity and made him a poet. Therefore he could love only her and would never forget her; he could never love **anyone** else, and yet he could only long for her constantly. She was incorporated into his own Self, and the memory of her was forever fresh. She had meant a lot to him; she had made him a poet, and by that very act she had signed her own death sentence. (J.V.) 3

It is not my intention to interpret <u>Repetition</u> in its entirety, merely to point to its introductory part where the concept of recurrence is outlined. Kierkegaard's so-called poetic existence may partake of both the demonic and the aesthetic, and the relationship between memory and recurrence creates an ambivalence in the aesthetic category itself, namely that of loss of identity, "empty noise", coupled with potential transcendence into a mythopoetic state that anticipates integration and emancipation, or at least contains a dormant or latent transcendence. The demonic category is so prevalent, however, that it becomes impossible to ignore its negative influence. The demonic is expressed, for example, in James Joyce's <u>A Portrait</u> and <u>Ulysses</u>, and in Tom Kristensen's <u>Havoc</u>, as psycho-sexual and social fixations, paralyses, that are not transcended; we can even designate the structure of these novels as "repetition", in the sense "empty noise", i.e., demonic continuity in nothingness, although the literary form itself and the self-transcendence of the Modernist consciousness can be seen to be emancipatory and conducive to a <u>semblance</u> of meaning. Kierkegaard says that the demonic reveals itself <u>incognito</u> only, and it is possible to see the symbol- and image-making activity of the three works as the incognito revelation of the demonic, its inverted image, rather than as emancipated resymbolization, or re-creation of identity; in other words, the aesthetic existence of the artist-hero is a symbolic construct, an extended mirror-image of fixation, and the dialectic between poetic symbol and psychic paralysis remains static, non-evolving, so that identity and continuity are lost. The novels express the "continuity of nothingness" that Kierkegaard speaks of in The Concept of Anxiety. Revelation is turned into mystification, a possibly apt description of Modernism itself, and the re-integration of Death and Eros is aborted, in these three novels at least, so that we can describe these particular literary experiments as an aesthetic of repetition without continuity.

The static nature of Irish society is reflected and conceptualized in James Joyce's aesthetic theory, as it is formulated by Stephen Dedalus in A Portrait of the Artist as a Young Man (1916). The reader is confronted with a dual motion of poetic generation and production: the reflection of a static, paralytic social condition, the immovable, conservative essence of Irish culture, religion, and politics; and the artist's reaction formation, i.e., the creation of a static, autonomous theory of art, an aesthetic projection of object cathexis, so to speak, the total <u>isolation</u> of the aesthetic object and its endowment with "divine" significance, radiance. Through this process, art itself becomes artificiality, attenuated from the potentially dynamic nature of reality; art becomes self-sufficient, and the artistic consciousness produces without purpose, without dynamic motion, and it is conscious of its own motion as it is, ultimately, divided from itself and impersonalized. The lack of individual, concrete autonomy in the subjective and in the sociopolitical world is compensated for by the creation of an autonymous imagination whose only purpose is the production of stylistic and structural variations. The development from <u>A</u> <u>Portrait</u> via <u>Ulysses</u> to <u>Finnegans</u> <u>Wake</u> runs from the personal, semi-autobiographical narrative via an artificial, literary balance between the personal and the aesthetic, to the complete artifact. The totally abstract artifact is anticipated in <u>A</u> <u>Portrait</u>, which forms the sociopolitical and literary thesis upon which the later works are based. Joyce's attitude is that he has no attitude, especially in regard to the political events of the time, including the internal affairs of Ireland. His consciousness abstracts from the events of the day, creates distance from them, and seeks an identity on a purely abstract, objective basis in an effort to achieve an aesthetic <u>unio</u> <u>mystica</u>, a higher synthesis of subject of object, a re-integration in the world of art that can replace the lost and only "remembered" individual and social identity that Stephen never establishes in <u>A Portrait</u>.

The novel is an account of the artist's personal history as a background for the poetic impetus that necessitates the view of the artistic object as being totally separate from society. Stephen states, in the last part of <u>A Portrait</u>, that the net of religion is laid out to catch his independent spirit, and that he intends to fly by all the nets of Irish culture. His personal abstraction from the nets of the Irish matrix - which include his mother, Irish Catholicism, the Gaelic League, Irish politics - assumes the form of a highly speculative aesthetic theory based on St. Thomas. Stephen's presentation of the theory is dually interspersed with Lynch's earthy remarks.

> In order to see that basket, said Stephen, your mind first of all separates the basket from the rest of the visible universe which

is not the basket. The first phase of apprehension is a bounding line drawn about the object to be apprehended. An esthetic image is presented to us either in space or in time. What is audible is presented in time, what is visible is presented in space. But, temporal or spatial, the esthetic image is first luminously apprehended as selfbounded and self-contained upon the immeasurable background of space or time which is not it. You apprehend it as *one* thing. You see it as one whole. You apprehend its wholeness. That is *integritas*.

— Bull's eye! said Lynch, laughing. Go on.

— Then, said Stephen, you pass from point to point, led by its formal lines; you apprehend it as balanced part against part within its limits; you feel the rhythm of its structure. In other words the synthesis of immediate perception is followed by the analysis of apprehension. Having first felt that it is *one* thing you feel now that it is a *thing*. You apprehend it as complex, multiple, divisible, separable, made up of its parts, the result of its parts and their sum, harmonious. That is *consonantia*.

— Bull's eye again! said Lynch wittily. Tell me now what is *claritas* and you win the cigar.

— The connotation of the word, Stephen said, is rather vague. Aquinas uses a term which seems to be inexact. It baffled me for a long time. It would lead you to believe that he had in mind symbolism or idealism, the supreme quality of beauty being a light from some other world, the idea of which the matter is but the shadow, the reality of which it is but the symbol. I thought he might mean that *claritas* is the artistic discovery and representation of the divine purpose in anything or a force of generalisation which would make the esthetic image a universal one, make it outshine its proper conditions. But that is literary talk. I understand it so. When you have apprehended that basket as one thing and have then analysed it according to its form and apprehended it as a thing you make the only synthesis which is logically and esthetically permissible. You see that it is

> that thing which it is and no other thing.
> The radiance of which he speaks is the scho-
> lastic *quidditas*, the *whatness* of a thing.
> This supreme quality is felt by the artist
> when the esthetic image is first conceived in
> his imagination. The mind in that mysterious
> instant Shelley likened beautifully to a
> fading coal. The instant wherein that supreme
> quality of beauty, the clear radience of the
> esthetic image, is apprehended luminously by
> the mind which has been arrested by its whole-
> ness and fascinated by its harmony is the
> luminous silent stasis of esthetic pleasure,
> a spiritual state very like to that cardiac
> condition which the Italian physiologist
> Luigi Galvani, using a phrase almost as
> beautiful as Shelley's, called the enchantment
> of the heart.[4]

The "silent stasis of esthetic pleasure", i.e., the intellection of the properties of the aesthetic object, corresponds to the stages of human perception itself. The two-way process is entirely abstract and intellectual and is meant to synthesize reality, subject and object, by abstracting from and purifying its dynamic essence, the changing and evolving aspect of the social world that Stephen fails to come to terms with during the narrative. His relationship to E.C., his loved one, is one example of his inner fragmentation, the split between the physical, instinctual, and the intellectual, and of his progressive alienation from the social world, which he does not understand and coldly rejects.

Rude brutal anger routed the last lingering instant of ecstasy from his soul. It broke up violently her fair image and flung the fragments on all sides. On all sides distorted reflections of her image started from his memory: the flowergirl in the ragged dress with damp coarse hair and a hoyden's face who had called herself his own girl and begged his handsel, the kitchengirl in the next house who sang over the clatter of her plates with the drawl of a country singer the first bars of *By Killarney's Lakes and Fells*, a girl who had laughed gaily to see him stumble when the iron grating in the footpath near Cork Hill had caught the broken sole of his shoe, a girl he had glanced at, attracted by her small ripe mouth as she passed out of Jacob's biscuit factory, who had cried to him over her shoulder:

— Do you like what you seen of me, straight hair and curly eyebrows?

And yet he felt that, however he might revile and mock her image, his anger was also a form of homage. He had left the classroom in disdain that was not wholly sincere, feeling that perhaps the secret of her race lay behind those dark eyes upon which her long lashes flung a quick shadow. He had told himself bitterly as he walked through the streets that she was a figure of the womanhood of her country, a batlike soul waking to the consciousness of itself in darkness and secrecy and loneliness, tarrying awhile, loveless and sinless, with her mild lover and leaving him to whisper of innocent transgressions in the laticed ear of a priest.[5]

The decomposition of "her fair image" is related to an inability to cope with sexuality, and to a reductive perception of woman whose "batlike soul" is "waking to the consciousness of itself in darkness and secrecy and loneliness". It is this solitary consciousness that

Stephen is imbued with himself, as an artist, as he identifies himself with the arch-rebel, Lucifer, "brightness" <u>falling</u> from the sky. Stephen's statement that he wishes to "forge" the "uncreated conscience of his race"[6] in silence, exile and cunning, identifies him with the secret consciousness of the Irish woman, and with the Satanic rebel who fell to a inverted replica of Heaven, a static reproduction of perfection as emptiness and boredom. Stephen is, of course, striving for perfection in the aesthetic image, and that kind of perfection is only possible in the realm of what Lukacs calls "abstract potentiality". It is significant that E.C., Stephen's clandestine love, is unconsciously identified with this "uncreated conscience", introjected, as she is, into Stephen's creative imagination, internalized as the sexual aspect of creativity. She becomes the inspirational force of his psyche, and he relates to her aesthetically as to a poetic muse who induces the life of the imagination into him. E.C. is, then, transformed into a mythopoetic consciousness which strongly wakens to "consciousness of itself in loneliness". Stephen exemplifies the progressive alienation of the artist, the humanistic subject, who performs an abstract dialectic by subsuming sexual and social "other" and incorporating it into his consciousness, re-making it into an artistic nucleus. By incorporating E.C.'s sexuality and her separate identity, Stephen utilizes, in a demonic fashion, the instinctual, libidinal powers of his own subconscious to an aesthetic end, as <u>will to art</u>. E.C. is injected into his mind where she is fused with aesthetic activity itself. Stephen controls sexual and social reality in this manner; he unites with it, and transcends it, aesthetically, and his aesthetic theory reflects the fundamental disparity between the artist and society; the theory also reflects the historical situation which is rooted in the Capitalist mode of production, and which has forced the artist to become dissociated from his culture. Stephen, and Joyce, are part of the historical process of alienation.

Stephen's personal history is delineated as a Hegelian dialectic of subject and object, a continuous progression from thesis and antithesis to synthesis. Each part of the novel poses an unresolved dichotomy between the young man and his environment, and each chapter ends on a note of temporary reconciliation and resurrection. The synthesis, however, is dissolved at the beginning of each new chapter; the temporary reconciliation is seen to be illusory and treated ironically by the author. Reconciliation is achieved, for example, at the end of part two:

> With a sudden movement she bowed his head and joined her lips to his and he read the meaning of her movements in he frank uplifted eyes. It was too much for him. He closed his eyes, surrendering himself to her, body and mind, conscious of nothing in the world but the dark pressure of her softly parting lips. They pressed upon his brain as upon his lips as though they were the vehicle of a vague speech; and between them he felt an unknown and timid pressure, darker than the swoon of sin, softer than sound or odour.[7]

The ecstacy of love and sexual union is immediately contradicted and negated in part three:

> The dull light fell more faintly upon the page whereon another equation began to unfold itself slowly and to spread abroad its widening tail. It was his own soul going forth to experience, unfolding itself sin by sin, spreading abroad the balefire of its burning stars and folding back upon itself, fading slowly, quenching its own lights and fires. They were quenched: and the cold darkness filled chaos.
> A cold lucid indifference reigned in his soul. At his first violent sin he had felt a wave of vitality pass out of him and had feared to find his body or his soul maimed by the excess. Instead the vital wave had carried him on its bosom out of himself and back again when it receded: and no part of body or soul had been maimed but a dark peace had been established between them. The chaos in which his ardour extinguished itself was a cold indifferent knowledge of himself.[8]

Stephen's temporary union with other, the synthesis of subject and object, is disrupted by his own cold indifference; the indifferent attitude evolves into a stasis of the mind, which Stepehn describes later,[9] and into impersonalization.

> The personality of the artist, at first a cry or a cadence or a mood and then a fluid and lambent narrative, finally refines itself out of existence, impersonalises itself, so to speak. The esthetic image in the dramatic form is life purified in and reprojected from the human imagination. The mystery of esthetic like that of material creation is accomplished. The artist, like the God of the creation, remains within or behind or beyond or above his handiwork, invisible, refined out of existence, indifferent, paring his fingernails.[10]

The process of impersonalization by which life is purified and "reprojected from the human imagination" creates the existential distance necessary to produce an art that is absolved from the painful involvement with changing personal and social relationships. This impersonalization is the cause of Stephen's refusal, in part five, to sign a petition for world peace, and of his growing distance from mother and country on the whole. The sociopolitical context of his conscious, aesthetic distance is indirectly inserted into the narrative as the author's, Joyce's, self-conscious judgment of himself as a kind of demonic consumer of social and sexual material to an aesthetic end. The world exists, for him, to be transposed into an abstract, literary realm, and the social and erotic tensions and fragmentations serve as fuel for a purely aesthetic re-integration that does not become a liberation, since the world is merely transposed, not transformed. The aesthetic symbol itself becomes a demonically inverted mirror image of psycho-sexual fixations and social paralysis. The hope for a new art, the hope of creating or "forging", ambiguously, the "uncreated conscience" of humankind, becomes exactly that: forgery, an aesthetic sublimation of personal experience, rather than a kinetic integration of self and other, as in Hunger. Joyce's next work, Ulysses, becomes a "disappointed bridge".

Joyce's aesthetic theory, intended to "forge" the "uncreated conscience", is thus based on three principles: the "arrest" of the mind that perceives and confronts the aesthetic object, stasis; the impersonalization of the artist, i.e., the objectification of the subjective, lyrical mode, the transmutation of personal experience to aesthetic life; and the reprojection of the poetic image from the soul of the artist. These principles express an attempt to recapture objective reality through the creative process and to communicate with it in the abstract realm of the poetic imagination, where the static matter of reality is transposed into static imagery. Stephen's identification with Lucifer, Icaros, and Dedalos, maker of the labyrinth, is indicative of the mythifying process by which he tries to absolve himself from the fragmented reality around him, and by which he tries to make a detour around the subject-object conflict which is most apparent in his relationship to women, who are split into the double image of the whore and the virgin. The "sanctification" of the poetic image passes through the demonic stage of sexual debasement and division, a process by which the cultural matrix, the maternal super-id, that was re-created in the personal vision of <u>Hunger</u>, is endowed with negative sexual energy, a negative cathexis of the id that is sublimated into art, to be sure, but which ultimately reflects the fragmentation of the artist's soul itself, its alienation from the social culture and from self, from spirit. The poetic images are forced into an undissolable relationship to the "nightmare of the past", the traditions of mother, church, and country; these social, political, and cultural entities are not interpreted from the perspective of change and evolution but viewed as stasis, as paralyzed self-division. The phenomena of social and psychological realities are captured, but the dynamic essence, the projection of historical change and of a second reality is not attained. Hamsun's hero was able to integrate with the cultural matrix because his art was the incarnation of personal experience; Joyce's hero, Stephen, formulates an aesthetic theory that is a philosophicoliterary symptom of the political stalemate of Irish society as he saw it, its poverty, its lack of social evolution, its religious conservatism, and its subservience to England.

During the course of the narrative, Stephen slowly disassociates himself from his family; he disagrees with his mother's religion and politics, and the familial ties disintegrate as the father deteriorates into a sentimentalist and a pauper. Stephen's own interpretation of his "flight" to Paris as a "disappointed bridge" points to an unresolved Oedipal conflict, when the absence of a strong father figure has created a freedom that Stephen cannot cope with. In place of the father image, Stephen incorporates various mythical figures, e.g. Icaros and Lucifer, who become ego-ideals, arch-rebels of his soul, emblems of his escape from Irish tyranny, and emblems of poetic sublimation; the sublimation, however, is a mythopoetic reprojection of regressed material that is not adequately comprehended. The re-sexualization of the Oedipal conflict, in Stephen's case, means the utilization of sexual, demonic powers to an aesthetic end; the sexual powers create the will to art in Joyce and determine his conscious choice of an aesthetic existence rather than a personal one. Joyce's modernistic consciousness is, of course, parallel to the general modernist tendency to produce art consciously and at a distance from society and self, through the process of impersonalization. This objective consciousness is the *sine qua non* for Joyce's literary production, and it creates its own paradoxical irony by being aware of its irreducible link to societal and personal imprisonment, its unfreedom. The demonic reproduction, the aesthetic repetition in the artistic object of a static situation, is the ironic reflection in art of a paralyzed social reality, because the will to art supersedes the will to change.

Stephen wants, of course, to transcend the static situation, and we can speak of an emancipatory process to the extent that "Irish material", i.e., the "uncreated conscience", is lifted to awareness of itself in the impersonal mind of the author who, perhaps, makes the reader conscious of his own culture. It is clear to me, however, that creation of new meaning does not occur, and that the hermeneutical process is confined to a partial deciphering. Joyce creates a demonic repetition of empty noise, the continuity of nothingness, in Kierkegaard's words: <u>Continuitet i Intet</u>.[11]

The aesthetic reproduction or reprojection of a static reality forms the artistic principle behind <u>Ulysses</u> (1922). This reprojection contradicts the Thomesian <u>consonantia</u> which Stephen conceptualized as the essence of his aesthetic theory, and it becomes clear that <u>Ulysses</u>, in its form and content, represents Icaros' fall from the sky; God himself turns into a noise in the street, a meaningless expression of the elemental matter of reality, reality as empty noise. With the fall of Icaros back to earth, the harmonious poetic image returns to the primal, sordid matter of social reality, the pre-linguistic sphere, and the social and interpersonal fragmentation of the communication process is injected into Stephen's ontological concept of the human condition, thus giving birth to what Lukacs calls an abstract particularity, i.e., an accurate, but disconnected and discontinuous presentation of reality and the subject's relation to it. The fall of Icaros thus aborts the process of resymbolization, by which the subject is integrated with the cultural matrix, and the Thomesian <u>consonantia</u> that was tenuous in the first place, returns to its original, inorganic state. We are forced to view the harmonious poetic image as an anachronistic attempt to apply scholastic philosophy to 20th century problems.

In terms of Stephen's socialization process, I see him as being saturated with the culture he rejects, as being forced back to it, inevitably. Through primary socialization, Stephen had internalized his society, had come into subjective possession of self and world. The formulation of the aesthetic theory represents, from this sociological point of view, a tenuous perceptual superposition, designed to create the "negative" that Marcuse interprets as a second reality, a narcissistic re-integration with the maternal super-id in the pre-Oedipal stage of development. The intellectual, speculative formulation of the aesthetic theory can be seen as an attempt to superimpose a secondary socialization process, the call of an artistic vocation, upon the primary socialization process; primary socialization persists, however, because of the complex nature of the subject-object conflict and the conscious abstraction from it through the will to art; Stephen's cold rejection of his own culture and of the potential in art to produce political change turns into aesthetic repetition of the cultural pattern he is saturated with. In Hunger the re-integration of poet and cultural matrix was personal and transcended the social limits of the self; in A Portrait, the re-integration is purely aesthetic, and the self is brought back to its own social limitations in Ulysses which exemplifies the aesthetic of repetition.

In the "Proteus" episode of Ulysses, Stephen is walking along the beach, reading the "signatures of all things".

> Ineluctable modality of the visible: at least that if no more, thought through my eyes. Signatures of all things I am here to read, seaspawn and seawrack, the nearing tide, that rusty boot. Snotgreen, blue-silver, rust: coloured signs. Limits of the diaphane. But he adds: in bodies. Then he was aware of them bodies before of them coloured. How? By knocking his sconce against them, sure. Go easy. Bald he was and a millionaire, *maestro di color che sanne*. Limit of the diaphane in. Why in? Diaphane, adiaphane. If you can put your five fingers through it, it is a gate, not a door. Shut your eyes and see.
> Stephen closed his eyes to hear his boots crush crackling wrack and shells. You are walking through it howsomever. I am, a stride at a time. A very short space of time through very short times of space. Five, six: the *nacheinander*. Exactly: and that is the

> ineluctable modality of the audible. Open
> your eyes. No. Jesus! If I fell over a
> cliff that beetles o'er his base, fell
> through the *nebeneinander* ineluctably. I
> am getting on nicely in the dark. My ash
> sword hangs at my side. Tap with it:
> they do. My two feet in his boots are at
> the end of his legs, *nebeneinander*. Sounds
> solid: made by the mallet of *Los Demiurgos*.
> Am I walking into eternity along Sandymount
> strand? Crush, crack, crick, crick. Wild
> sea money.[12]

The Proteus of Stephen's intellect struggles to reveal the essence of reality behind the changing faces of reality, first through the ineluctable modality of the visible. Aristotle was aware of reality as body prior to color, so Stephen closes his eyes to perceive the ineluctable modality of the audible, but perceives only the nacheinander, the temporal form, as the manifestations of phenomena; essence eludes him, reality becomes Protean and disintegrates into flux. The maternal culture has degenerated to the base, material element of the "snotgreen" sea, which Stephen repeatedly refuses to bathe in. The fragmentation of the maternal element in this episode is a reprojection of the fragments of "her fair image", the image of woman which was angrily flung to all sides in A Portrait. The only synthesizing function of the episode is the often lyrical cadence of the individual phrase which produces a formal superimposition, a paradoxically harmonious form of the particular that is contradicted, however, by the non-structure of the total narrative content, an unstructured structure of repetition, a continuous presentation of identical images, symbols and events throughout each episode that is "vainly released":

> Under the upswelling tide he saw the writhing weeds lift languidly and sway reluctant arms, hising up their petticoats, in whispering water swaying and upturning coy silver fronds. Day by day: night by night: lifted, flooded and let fall. Lord, they are weary: and, whispered to, they sigh. Saint Ambrose heard it, sigh of leaves and waves, waiting, awaiting the fullness of their times, *diebus ac noctibus iniurias patiens ingemiscit*. To no end gathered: vainly then released, forth flowing, wending back: loom of the moon. Weary too in sight of lovers, lascivious men, a naked woman shining in her courts, she draws a toil of waters.[13]

The fall of Lucifer is a fall towards the endlessly repeated cycle of death, organic matter returning to its inorganic state.

> Bag of corpsegas sooping in foul brine. A quiver of minnows, fat of a spongy titbit, flash through the slits of his buttoned trouserfly. God becomes man becomes fish becomes barnacle goose becomes featherbed mountain. Dead breaths I living breathe, tread dead dust, devour a urinous offal from all dead. Hauled stark over the gunwale he breathes upward the stench of his green grave, his leprous nosehole snoring to the sun.
> A seachange this, brown eyes saltblue. Seadeath, mildest of all deaths known to man. Old

> Father Ocean. *Prix de Paris:* beware of imi-
> tations. Just you give it a fair trial. We
> enjoyed ourselves immensely.
>   Come. I thirst. Clouding over. No black
> clouds anywhere, are there? Thunderstorm.
> Allbright he falls, proud lightning of the
> intellect, *Lucifer, dico, qui nescit occasum.*
> No. My cockle hat and staff and his my sandal
> shoon. Where? To evening lands. Evening
> will find itself.[14]

Stephen's creative activity descends to the level of urination, the only act by which he communes with the ocean of life: "It flows purling, widely flowing, floating foam pool, flower unfurling."[15]

The act of urination, "making water", as a travesty of creative activity is inserted into the modern commercialized communication process in the "Aeolus" episode, which takes place in the offices of the "Freeman's Journal", also called the "urinal". The quantification of reality that occurs in the pedestrian communication of everyday events is symbolized by the static motion of the newspaper printing press, which is the emblem of motion on the spot, empty noise; the episode is written in the style of inflated rhetoric. Anything of interest is printed, haphazardly, everything has equal value.

> It's the ads and side features sell a weekly
> not the stale news in the official gazette.
> Queen Anne is dead. Published by authority
> in the year one thousand and. Demesne situate
> in the townland of Rosenallis, barony of

> Tinnachinch. To all whom it may concern schedule pursuant to statute showing return of number of mules and jennets exported from Ballina. Nature notes. Cartoons. Phil Blake's weekly Pat and Bull story. Uncle Toby's page for tiny tots. Country bumpkin's queries. Dear Mr. Editor, what is a good cure for flatulence? I'd like that part. Learn a lot teaching others. The personal not M.A.P. Mainly all pictures. Shapely bathers on golden strand. World's biggest balloon. Double marriage of sisters celebrated. Two bridegrooms laughing heartily at each other. Cuprani too, printer. More Irish than the Irish.
> The machines clanked in threefour time. Thump, thump, thump. Now if he got paralysed there and no one knew how to stop them they'd clank on and on the same, print it over and over and up and back. Monkeydoodle the whole thing. Want a cool head.[16]

"Proteus" and "Aeolus" are inextricably linked through the identification of the phenomenology of perception with the act of public communication. The act of highly intellectual and poetic perception and the act of inflated public communication, originally conceived as two separate types of literary language, enter the common ground of fragmentation as the reader becomes aware of their focus on the disparate, discontinuous phenomena of life; this focus expresses the distortion of perception and of the linguistic process itself. The fragmented images of social and metaphysical phenomena become extensions of Stephen's, and Joyce's, unresolved Oedipal conflict, and of the alienation from parent and culture that occurs in post-industrial Capitalism. The class conflict is neutralized as the working class is slowly absorbed into the middle class, and political ideology is superseded by commercial interest, producing the equalization of value, as identity and essence become exchangeable "commodities", the fluctuating masks of Proteus; these masks are the incarnations of a temporal flux that obfuscates actual historical time and the dialectical process of societal change that is produced by the dynamic interplay between the autonomous subject and its milieu.

Stephen's problem with the parental authority figures manifests itself as an oppressive ego-ideal that subjects the ego to guilt, or, as Stephen calls it, "the agenbite of inwit"; guilt is associated with the past, and history becomes a "nightmare" from which Stephen tries to awake. The past is re-worked through memory, and the characters try to assimilate their personal history and the history of the culture with the present time; the product of this assimilation is the stream-of-consciousness technique, which presents character from the perspective of flux and dissolution. The sheer weight of the "guilty" past prevents the characters from forming an evolving personal history, a continuing identity; the past itself, then, assumes the function of a negative, "sadistic" ego-ideal which injects itself into the streaming thought of the heroes. Memory becomes "remembering backwards", rather than "remembering forward"; the past is repeated in the present, and this is the essence of what Joyce calls the Irish paralysis.

Backwards memory rather than future projection creates the style and tone of the "Penelope" episode. Everything in this episode is recollection of the past, a web or tapestry of memory and sense data with no apparent continuity.

> ... the sun shines for you he said the day we were lying among the rhododendrons on owth head in the grey tweed suit and his straw hat the day I got him to propose to me yes first I gave him the bit of seedcake out of my mouth and it was leapyear like now yes 16 years ago my God after that long kiss I near lost my breath yes he said I was a flower of the mountain yes so we are flowers all a womans body yes that was one true thing he said in his life and the sun shines for you today yes that was why I likes him because I saw he understood or felt what a woman is and I knew I could always get round him and I gave him all the pleasure I could leading him on till he asked me to say yes and I wouldnt answer first only looked out over the sea and the sky I was thinking of so many things he didnt know of Mulvey and Mr. Stanhope and Hester and father and old captain Groves and the sailors playing all birds fly and I say stoop and washing up dishes they called it on the pier and the sentry in front of the governors house with the thing round his white helmet poor devil half roasted and the Spanish girls laughing in their

shawls and their tall combs and the auctions
in the morning the Greeks and the jews and
the Arabs and the devil knows who else from
all ends of Europe and Duke street and the fowl
market all clucking outside Larby Sharons and
the poor donkeys slipping half asleep and the
vague fellows in the cloaks asleep in the shade
on the steps and the big wheels of the carts of
the bulls and the old castle thousands of years
old yes and those handsome Moors all in white
and turbans like kings asking you to sit down
in their little bit of a shop and Ronda with the
old windows of the posadas glancing eyes a
lattice hid for her lover to kiss the iron and
the wineshops half open at night and the casta-
nets and the night we missed the boat at Algeciras
the watchman going about serene with his lamp
and O that awful deepdown torrent O and the sea
the sea crunsib sometimes like fire and the
glorious sunsets and the figtrees in the Ala-
meda gardens yes and all the queer little streets
and pink and blue and yellow houses and the rose-
gardens and the jessamine and geraniums and cac-
tuses and Gibraltar as a girl where I was a
Flower of the mountain yes when I put the rose
in my hair like the Andalusian girls used or
shall I wear a red yes and how he kissed me
under the Moorish wall and I thought well as
well him as another and then I asked him with
my eyes to ask again yes and then he asked me
would I yes to say yes my mountain flower and
first I put my arms around him yes and drew him
down to me so he could feel my breasts all per-
fume yes and his heart was going like mad and
yes I said yes I will Yes.[17]

This final affirmation occurs in the past only, Molly's dreaming stream of thought. Her mode of consciousness exemplifies the Bergsonian flux of time, internal psychological time, ahistorical time. Joyce's concept of time, as it is manifested in the stream of consciousness, is an abstraction from historical time and divorced from the potential vision of a future society. The stream of consciousness becomes the most radical expression of dissolution, isolation, and subjectivity; the personal experience is absorbed totally into pure aesthetics, an abstract synthesis which becomes the aesthetic answer to painful personal problems. Subjectivity becomes a lyrical, streaming process as the artistic form is separated from social and individual identity, and character is "vainly released" into a fluid medium, the vehicle of a possible expansion of the ego.

Joyce also attempts to achieve such an expansion, in lieu of an actually evolving identity and personality structure, through the abolition of sexual difference, through the projection of an androgynous type, an eroticoreligious unio mystica. The "Circe" episode is the scene of projected androgeny, a suprasexual, "Platonic" union with religious and mystical overtones; Bloom, for example, is said to be happy because he is not a sexual conqueror, and because his relationship to Molly transcends sex. Joyce attempts to dissolve the identity of the characters and create a new form of the soul; this new form is embodied in dramatic characters who represent latent tendencies, and who attenuate the human personality from its previously fixed social and interpersonal relationships; the character of Leopold Bloom is dissolved, and a new "womanly man" appears, in the vestige of transsexuality, bisexuality, and androgeny. The scene takes place in a Dublin brothel presided over by Bella.

> DR MULLIGAN: *(In motor jerkin, green motor-goggles on his brow)* Dr Bloom is bisexually abnormal. He has recently escaped from Dr Eustace's private asylum for demented gentlemen. Born out of bedlock hereditary epilepsy is present, the consquence of unbridled lust. Traces of elephantiasis have been discovered among his ascendants. There are marked symptoms of chronic exhibitionism. Ambidexterity is also latent. He is prematurely bald from selfabuse, perversely idealistic in consequence, a reformed rake, and has metal teeth. In consequence of a family complex he has temporarily lost his memory and I believe him to more sinned against than sinning. I have made a pervaginal examination and, after application of the acid test to 5427 anal, axillary, pectoral, and pubic hairs, I declare him to be *virgo intacta*. *(Bloom holds his high grade hat over his genital organs)*[18]

Bloom turns female and subjects himself masochistically to Bella:

> BLOOM: *(Mumbles)* Awaiting your further orders, we remain, gentlemen . . .
> BELLO: *(With a hard basilisk stare, in a baritone voice)* Hound of dishonour!
> BLOOM: *(Infatuated)* Empress!
> BELLO: *(His heavy cheekchops sagging)* Adorer of the adulterous rump!
> BLOOM: *(Plaintively)* Hugeness!
> BELLO: Dungdevourer!
> BLOOM: *(With sinews semiflexed)* Magnificence.

BELLO: Down! *(He taps her on the shoulder with his fan)* Incline feet forward! Slide left foot one pace back. You will fall. You are falling. On the hands down.
BLOOM: *(Her eyes upturned in the sign of admiration, closing)* Truffles!
(With a piercing epileptic cry she sinks on all fours, grunting, snuffling, rooting at his feet, then lies, shamming dead with eyes shut tight, trembling eyelids, bowed upon the ground in the attitude of most excellent master)
BELLO: *(With bobbed hair, purple gills, fat moustache rings round his shaven mouth, in mountaineer's puttees, green silverbuttoned coat, sport skirt and alpine hat with moorcock's feather, his heel on her neck and grinds it in)* Feel my entire weight. Bow, bondslave, before the throne of your despot's glorious heels, so glistening in their proud erectness.
BLOOM: *(Enthralled, bleats)* I promise never to disobey.[19]

Bloom's androgynous identity as the new "womanly man" is mocked at, revealed as perversion; the sins of his past speak in unison, betraying his latent sexual deviance.

THE SINS OF THE PAST: *(In a medley of voices)* He went through a form of clandestine marriage with at least one woman in the shadow of the Black Church. Unspeakable messages he telephoned mentally to Miss Dunn at an address in d'Olier Street while he presented himself indecently to the instrument in the callbox. By word and deed he encouraged a nocturnal strumpet to deposit fecal and other matter in an unsanitary outhouse attached to empty premises. In five public conveniences he wrote pencilled messages offering his nuptial partner to all strongmembered males. And by the offensively smelling vitriol works did he not pass night after night by loving courting courting couples to see if and what and how

much he could see? Did he not lie in bed, the
gross boar, gloating over a nauseous fragment
of wellused toilet paper presented to him by
a nasty harlot, stimulated by gingerbread and
a postal order?[20]

Bloom passes through an entire catalogue of sexual
aberrations, as he is changed into a "swine", much like
Odysseus' men in the Homeric parallel; and Stephen
Dedalus' guilt feelings towards his mother, who is
"beastly" dead, are unfolded in a nightmarish vision:

>   STEPHEN: *Ah non, par exemple!* The intellec-
>   tual imagination! With me all or not at all.
>   *Non serviam!*
>   FLORRY: Give him some cold water. Wait.
>   *(She rushes out)*
>   THE MOTHER: *(Wrings her hands slowly, moaning
>   desperately)* O Sacred Heart of Jesus, have
>   mercy on him! Save him from hell, O divine
>   Sacred Heart!
>   STEPHEN: No! No! No! Break my spirit all of
>   you if you can! I'll bring you all to heel!
>   THE MOTHER: *(In the agony of her deathrattle)*
>   Have mercy on Stephen, Lord, for my sake! In-
>   expressible was my anguish when expiring with
>   love, grief and agony on Mount Calvary.
>   STEPHEN: *Nothung!*
>   *(He lifts his ashplant high with both hands
>   and smashes the chandelier. Time's livid
>   final flame leaps and, in the following
>   darkness, ruin of all space, shattered glass
>   and toppling masonry.)*
>   THE GASJET: Pwfungg!
>   BLOOM: Stop!
>   LYNCH: *(Rushes forward and seizes Stephen's
>   hand)* Here! Hold on! Don't run amok!
>   BELLA: Police!
>   *(Stephen, abandoning his ashplant, his head and
>   arms thrown back stark, beats the ground and
>   flees from the room past the whores at the door)*[21]

Stephen's nihilistic act which follows immediately upon the apparition of his horribly dead mother, relates the creative act itself to destruction and death, the shattering of all space, and Lucifer's words "non serviam" reflect the inversion of the rebellious spirit of art, its compulsive relation to mental fixations and past psychological history; in this case, the "nightmare of history" speaks with the "clamor of death" and guilt and reveals an Oedipus complex which overshadows the conscious life of the artist-protagonist (Stephen) and makes him engage in a morbidly repetitious act of negative tribute to the maternal culture, i.e., the writing of <u>Ulysses</u>. The introjection of the maternal bond produces a resexualization of the Oedipal conflict that vents itself as a negative attraction to the mother figure and what she represents. Stephen's, and Joyce's, art stays within the confines of Irish culture by impulsion, and the spiritual union of Leopold Bloom, Stephen Dedalus, and Molly Bloom, is aborted and broken down to the rudimentary fractions of semi-pathological behavior. The vision of the unio mystica is abandoned as sexual deliverance turns into sexual bondage, an inevitable link with the past. The attempt to create a new form of the soul, a modern typology beyond fixed, conditioned personal and social relationships, is shipwrecked due to the fundamentally deterministic view of human nature and culture that is imbedded in the Irish paralysis which Joyce's art is about. The only release is achieved through comedy, the genre Ulysses belongs to.

Irony operates as the "incognito" of the implied author in Havoc (1930). The dialectic between author and protagonist is the expression of the hero's approximation to the central, authorial perspective, which he, little by little, is forced to adopt. The author's insight, his pre-awareness, manifests itself in the anticipatory preface, "Fear the soul and do not cultivate it for it resembles a vice". Ole Jastrau's quest is a search for this soul, a form of expanded self that he calls the "eternal soul", a phrase that makes us suspect, already at the outset, the illusory and regressive nature of his soul-searching. The "eternal soul" is a reference to the explosive subjective form of 1890's lyricism and to Nietzsche's deep eternity, the Dionysean timelessness of the human spirit that has expanded beyond restricting social and psychological limits. Jastrau's increasing, evolving self-irony precipitates his involvement with the central ironic perspective of the narrative as the "eternal soul" turns into the "impossible soul",

a phrase coined by Jastrau himself. The awareness of
the futility of the quest is immanent from the beginning,
as Jastrau's serious self-image is contrasted with the
image of his fleshy, "Mongolian" face in the bathroom
mirror. The mirror, and the window, is on the whole
used symbolically as an impenetrable wall that both
reflects the "ineluctable modality" of the soul, so to
speak, and prevents the hero from "expanding" or developing beyond his own self; the self has already been
defined, and Jastrau's attempts to recapture the creative, poetic spirit of his youth are shipwrecked, as
they turn into mirage and drunkenness. Only when drunk
does Jastrau experience feelings of a liberated self,
the feelings he had when he was a young poet, an Expres-
sionist. The autobiographical element is obvious here,
as we have a reference to Tom Kristensen's own Expressionistic poetry which culminated in the decade between
1920 and 1930. Havoc closes this poetic era for
good and can thus be seen to contain an element of literary self-evaluation, an evaluation of the premis for
art, a stage James Joyce had passed through long ago as
he made the conscious choice to "write his life" instead
of living it.

Ole Jastrau eventually discovers the last (vice) at the bottom of his soul, a basic immovability which becomes the foundation for the tenuous symbolic values and for the repetitive narrative structure, the literary representation of societal paralysis. Unlike Ulysses which represents a conscious choice of art over life, Havoc retains the personal problematic as something intrinsic to the novel, that which the novel is about. The personal problematic, the evolving dialectic between individual and environment, shapes the greater part of Havoc, as it did in A Portrait; both novels become a literary history of the progressive alienation of the humanistic subject, but the conclusions vary: Stephen Dedalus decides to "forge" his art, whereas Ole Jastrau gives up writing poetry. Jastrau's future history lies outside the fictional frame of the novel, in an extra-literary space; Joyce's and Stephen's development creates an abstract literary space, an extra-social space, which transcends the personal problematic and evades psychological and political solutions. The ultimate irony of Ulysses, as we have seen, is that the minute linguistic units, phrases and paragraphs, create a musical, pleasing contrast to the earthly matter of the content. The structure of Havoc also transcends content in an

artificial manner, as the novel form is contrasted to
the fragmentation of Jastrau's soul and as it develops
a consistent superimposition of aesthetic patterns, re-
curring symbols and images, on top of the social and
personal chaos. However, the aesthetic form itself, and
the symbolic values, slowly "falls to the ground" as it
is invalidated by the negative psychosocial content of
the novel. The soul falls, and so do the symbolic values
that express that soul, and the quest of the hero, who
is also a writer, deteriorates into empty repetition,
mechanical, static movement. Jastrau becomes an imita-
tion of himself, and events repeat themselves endlessly
(the only "eternal" element in the novel!) and turn into
the hell of the demonic category, continuity in nothingness.
Poetic self-expansion becomes alcoholism as Jastrau goes
to the same bars and wakes up in the same hotels. The
novel form is, therefore, an aesthetic abstraction that
is questioned in the novel content itself; this questioning creates the intrinsic action of the narrative
and absorbs the dynamic energy of the creative process.
The questioning activity, then, replaces and precludes
the creation of a significant "negative", the projection
of a future society and a new personality. The literary
activity of Ulysses and Havoc, the creative produc-

tivity itself, is self-directed, introverted. It is about itself.

Jastrau's search for the "eternal soul", the expanded ego-state, commences as a break with the restrictive aspects of his life, his family and his career as a literary critic at the major Copenhagen newspaper, "Dagbladet". Jastrau's slow, conscious "divorce" from his restraining social context parallels Kierkegaard's emphasis on the subjective absolute as the only way to fulfill the need for self-realization; the perception of the 19th century philosopher and the 20th century literary artist is the same: the social world is too narrow to contain the personal self and its search for meaning. The difference between the two is to be found, not in this identical premis, but in the concluding step: Kierkegaard creates meaning by choosing the subjective absolute; Kristensen loses meaning through his inability to synthesize and integrate the fragments of consciousness, through his inability to "write poetry", i.e., find a vehicle which adequately expresses and actualizes the longing self. The deepest irony of Jastrau's escape from the social world is that the soul he searches for is itself socially conditioned, moulded into a rigid form that reflects the social and cultural rigidity around him. Jastrau's inability to write poetry is an expression of his developmental paralysis and his lack of actual autonomy.

Prior to Jastrau's leaving his newspaper career for good, the chief editor, Iversen, tries to tempt him to stay by evoking the very object of journalism itself, the dynamic, pulsating life of the city. He takes Jastrau to the window which overlooks a large square, and points to the street.

> It was a strangely unsteady, flickering moment. Jastrau would always remember the square outside as it lay stretched out in front of him now, a mild and white surface, sloping like an ocean viewed from an incline, and he would remember the dark stream of people crossing the square, constant movement, all those bright, bright women. And suddenly the figure of the large, stooping, dull-eyed editor and the lively square down there merged in one image: journalism, intensely alive, yet tired and disillusioned. (J.V.) 22

The vivacious activity in the street below blends with the editor's tired, lifeless facial expression; the editor's lifelessness is a manifestation of the futile attempt to fill out the superficial, "sensational" life below with meaning through language. Iversen has spent himself, as a career journalist, to an empty, aesthetic end, and the dynamic vitality of the street is no more than the projected product of newspaper sensationalism, inflated rhetoric, as in the "Aeolus" episode of Ulysses. The arch-temptor, in the guise of the chief editor, beckons to Jastrau in an effort to deceive him with the superficial beauty of an exterior scene. The newspaper becomes emblematic of all creative activity: it symbolizes the final deflation, the de-valuation of language itself, as ideas and values are put up for sale and consumption in the columns of the paper. Language becomes deficient in a double sense: it receives and duplicates external information unrealistically, sensationally; and it projects meaning into scenes and events that do not carry meaning. The latter futile function of language represents the nadir of Tom Kristensen's own Expressionistic phase: intense internal matter is being projected into an empty space.

After Jastrau's chosen disassociation from the social world, emphasis is placed on a subjective, psychological experience that reflects, increasingly, the adult character's compulsion to repeat early sexual patterns and complexes. Ole Jastrau's soul is revealed as the battleground of the ambivalent forces of psychic fixation and psychic expansion. Jastrau expands into the private cosmos of the soul; his apartment becomes a projection of this expansion, as furniture is moved away from the center of the floor, as Steffensen and Anna Marie move in.

Jastrau stared at him. He had experienced that answer, that discussion once before. No, this dark room facing north, the sunny facade on the other side of the street, this ghostlike afternoon, these two people, the music from the recordplayer, ceaseless, ceaseless, and beer bottles on the table, beer caps lying around, no, never could he have experienced this before. But suddenly the surroundings changed, assuming an imperishable form before his eyes. These two faces. This starved, fanatical student, for Steffensen was - was a student, that and nothing else, an insane student; and this servant girl who had no idea what to do with her body or her soul!
And again Jastrau was sitting at the head of the table, bringing his hands together as if he wanted to break bread. Emaus! Sitting in that position he understood everything, he thought, and had faith in his own inner light.
But Steffensen continued:
"An image. You see, I've always felt that this whole apartment was floating in the air." He gulped down some beer. " As soon as I came in here, everything would rise up in the air. The apartment, these rooms, would sail - like a heavenly ship, you know - and that's what it's doing now. Especially when we are playing jazz music, ha. And now I am convinced that everything will stay suspended - up high, Jastrau, high above the whole filthy mess - if we - we are the passengers - what shall I say - if we let everything happen, everything. That is, if we let infinity rule. But .... "
Jastrau leaned forward, staring at Steffensen's pale, ravaged face, the high sinister forehead, the shining eyes, and the mechanical mouth. Yes, he was insane. This last winter had left its mark on him. But the thought, the image, moved him even more intensely than this paralyzed face.
"Yes, I understand," Jastrau replied, as Steffensen looked at him anxiously. "All decaying things convey a feeling of infinity." (J.V.) 23

The apartment is like a "heavenly ship" floating in eternity; the explosion, or implosion, of symbolic content extends the nature of the three characters to the suprahuman, and Jastrau is identified with Christ, the fusion of the human and the divine. He is breaking bread at the end of the table and sees himself as possessed by an inner light. His kinship to Stephen and Anna Marie becomes mystical, but the spirituality of this union, which contains an echo of the "trinity" of Bloom, Stephen, and Molly in *Ulysses*, falls to the ground as we learn that Anna Marie and Steffensen carry a syphilitic infection that forces them to abstain from sex. The "spirituality" has a purely physiological origin; it is determined, not free.

Steffensen wants to transcend his own biological and social fate; both Stefan and Jastrau have a personal history containing a fateful relationship to a parent: Jastrau lost his mother when he was three, made her into a Madonna figure, and has never been able to integrate the Madonna and the sexual woman. Stefan hates his father, rejects him because of his religious hypocrisy and political conservatism. Stefan's father transmitted the syphilitic infection to Anna Marie, and the infection becomes symbolic of the deroute of language itself, its degeneracy. Stefan's own poetry becomes, by reaction, even more radical, politically and aesthetically, than Jastrau's youthful Communist poems. Steffensen writes two contrasting, yet similar poems, the first of which is about <u>angst</u>.

> Boundless as Asia is fear.
> During untimely seasons it bloomed.
> And my blood carries ceaseless sensations
> of continents death-bound and doomed.
>
> But my fear is delivered through longing
> and through visions of terror and pain.
> I have longed for disasters and shipwrecks
> and for havoc and death gone insane.
>
> I have longed to see cities on fire
> and multitudes, mad, put to flight,
> revolutions, extreme, universal,
> and signs of God's wrath: earthquakes and blight. (J.V.) [24]

The movement of the poem is an internal falling through the soul, a continuous, but redundant expansion achieved through the superimposition of identical material that magnifies itself and finally bursts through the limits of the self, projecting the self-explosion on to an external, universal destruction; this destruction of the world is a form of deliverance of the self, a havoc of the soul, which is enigmatically based on a demonic eroticism that drives Steffensen's self towards a new form, the ethereal, the intangible. The violent images of this first poem are a preparation for the transformation of the physical to the intangible forms of "Diminuendo".

> Tired of loving you, happy, expended
> I live in a lingering kiss on your lips,
> feeling them fade in diminishing breath
> as your slumbering kiss into shapelessness slips.
>
> Tired of kissing, caressing I follow
> the contours of breasts and of thighs as I mould
> out of darkness a shimmering vase,
> bright as your body and light as your soul.
>
> Tired of touching, and feeling how tangibly
> ocean-calm loving has softened your form,
> now I look at your face that is capsized on pillows,
> your hair, tossed and tangled like seaweed by storm.
>
> Tired of seeing and feeling and loving you,
> away from your bed and your calm must I roam,
> feeling my way among things in your chamber,
> sensing you here in the stillness of home.
>
> Anna Marie, you live in all things,
> Anna Marie, so warm and so still,
> Anna Marie, I long for the coolness,
> Anna Marie, by the window so chill. (J.V.) [25]

The state of mind described here belongs to the realm of the wordless and becomes an expression of Stefan's wish to transcend the verbal, make poetry into pure will and action, and his desire to live like a mute animal. The self of the poem is attenuated from the ordinary vehicles of sexual expression and expands into an increasing formlessness, a fluid state which creates a marked contrast to Jastrau's "fluid state", his alcoholism. This new form of the soul is restless, however; it is achieved by giving up sexual gratification, by breaking the union of male and female, so that the poet's soul ends up outside the body and mind of its lover. Outside the window, which is at the end of the poem, is death and empty space.

The expansion of the soul can be conceptualized as an escape from internal bondage and fixation, e.g., Jastrau's fixation on the mother figure. The syphilitic infection symbolizes this internal bondage, a contamination that is passed on from generation to generation, and that infects language itself. At the center of Jastrau's soul is an immovable Fate - he is determined to be what he is; and Steffensen's eyes possess a hard radiance, like enamel. They reflect only his inner self, fixated and desperate, and are not directed towards the future. The self-expansion, and the symbolism surrouding it, falls to the ground because of its own dubious foundation. The untouchable woman becomes an extension of an internal immovability. The immovable center of Jastrau's soul creates only vertical movement, abstract image-making, not horizontal movement, action. The creation of a poetic vision actually prevents the characters from moving ahead in their lives. Furthermore, the demonic, undissolable paralysis at the center of the soul is connected with a fundamental carelessness about oneself and others. Kristensen is very close to Joyce's aesthetic choice, his escape from personal experience, and the origin of creative productivity is interpreted in the same way in Havoc and in A Portrait: poetic vision and symbolism are inescapably linked to a fixed content.

A strange happiness pervades the mood of Anna Marie and Jastrau as they walk through the Tivoli Gardens. I believe the happiness is due to the Platonic nature of the relationship. They are absolved from the normal, everyday restrictions of sexual relationships, and they have transcended, briefly, their social limitations. At this point, however, an image hits Jastrau as they are looking at some fish in an aquarium:

> Some large, red fish were chasing each other, snapping their soft mouths, and behind them there was a swarm of small, striped perch, a multitude of fish tails and fins in motion, while bubbles were fizzing up through the green, luminous water. A long, light-bodied eel was pending down through the aquarium like a plant stem.
> And one moment later Jastrau was as hypnotized as the other spectators by the gliding movements of the fish.
> Then a shock ran through him. In the middle of the tank a pearl-grey fish was poised, motionless, diagonal, its beak-like head close to the sandy bottom. A terrible force emanated from its obliviousness. It was aware of its own power.

> And now it was beyond comprehension that one had not seen it immediately. It made up the center, terrifying, immovable. And when it quickly flashed its eyes, one could feel it like an electric shock.
> It was a pike.
> "Why shall I never forget that, now?" said Jastrau. And they left. (J.V.) 26

The immovable fish, a demonic inversion of Christ, reminds Jastrau, finally, of his own repression and fixation, and it is also linked to the sociopolitical stagnation epitomized by the newspaper. The impact of the fish-image precipitates Jastrau's cynical self-discovery and propels him further into alcoholism. His attempt to find and expand his own naturalness as a human subject turns him, finally, into a subjekt,[27] as he wakes up in a park after an all night binge.

The "eternal soul" becomes the impossible soul, and recurrence, Kierkegaard's "gentagelse", is inverted to empty repetition. Kristensen and Joyce both interpret the origin of the creative process negatively, as an aesthetic rooted in an indissolable, demonic eroticism that is tied to unconscious social ideologies and illusions. The artist attempts to make these ideologies conscious and to transcend them, but they operate in the works as Fate. The novels do not go beyond this Fate, they do not project a second reality, a future for the protagonists and their societies. Meaning is not found, and the aesthetic form does not evolve into a "perceptual superposition" or a personal re-integration. It is only a temporary deliverance, and it returns to its own dubious source.

CHAPTER IV REFERENCES

[1] Søren Kierkegaard, Samlede Værker, Bd. 5. (København: Gyldendal, 1963), p. 115.

[2] Kierkegaard, p. 131.

[3] Kierkegaard, p. 121.

[4] James Joyce, A Portrait of the Artist as a Young Man. (New York: Penguin Books, 1976), pp. 212-213.

[5] Joyce, pp. 220-221.

[6] Joyce, p. 253.

[7] Joyce, p. 101.

[8] Joyce, p. 103.

[9] Joyce, p. 208.

[10] Joyce, p. 215.

[11] Kierkegaard, Samlede Værker, Bd. 6. (København: Gyldendal, 1963), p. 215.

[12] James Joyce, Ulysses, (London: The Bodley Head, 1960), p. 45.

[13] Joyce, Ulysses, pp. 62-63.

[14] Joyce, Ulysses, p. 63.

[15] Joyce, Ulysses, p. 62.

[16] Joyce, Ulysses, pp. 150-151.

[17] Joyce, Ulysses, pp. 931-933.

[18] Joyce, Ulysses, p. 613.

[19] Joyce, Ulysses, p. 644.

[20] Joyce, Ulysses, p. 649.

[21] Joyce, Ulysses, p. 682-683.

[22] Tom Kristensen, Hærværk, (København: Gyldendal, 1930), p. 288.

[23] Kristensen, pp. 248-249.

[24] Kristensen, p. 62.

[25] Kristensen, p. 148.

[26] Kristensen, p. 304.

[27] In Danish, "subjekt" means both "subject" and "bum".

CHAPTER 5

EROS AND TIME
AS I LAY DYING; THE DWARF; THE LIAR

Hermeneutic activity is the stimulation of creative memory and energy as the negation of the here and now, and the subsequent projection of Utopia, the creation of meaning as a revival of the past union of subject and object. In my discussion, I have distinguished between two kinds of memory, Kierkegaard's *erindring* and his concept of *gentagelse*, the former referring to a type of memory that is fixated on the past, discontinuous, and the latter referring to recollection in the sense of "remembering forward", in the sense of creative change and continuity. In the novel *Hunger* the two principles were seen to work consecutively; scattered memory and sense data posed a constant contradiction to the actual creative process that produced, on a partly subconscious level, a reintegration between subject and object, the individual's union with the maternal Eros, a reunion with unique political and ideological implications; the reunion establishes, namely, a transcendence of the alienation of Capitalism and of the sexual dualism; it creates new sexual politics and previses a society in which class divisions are annulled. The reunion with the maternal

Eros is, then, the specific political and psychological emblem of a recollected prehistoric happiness, or, in more strict Freudian terms, the evocation of the pre-Oedipal, narcissistic stage during which the pleasure principle operates at its fullest. The pre-Oedipal stage is, perhaps, the psychic equivalent of Marx's valorization of matriarchal communism, a prehistoric societal form that can be recollected and serve as the impetus for modern revolutionary action. Herbert Marcuse's work on hermeneutics takes the explicit form of a valorization of memory, or rather, recollection as <u>gentagelse</u>, and Kierkegaard's work on the concepts of freedom and time emphasizes equally much the existential and cultural importance of mnemosyne, the re-creative memory, that will liberate man and woman from time itself, "time" being a designation of the restricted temporality of personal and societal history. The implementation of this liberating form of recollection, the remembrance of a "temps perdu", may produce concrete social liberation in the sense of a reformation or revolution of historical forms and political processes. Freud's reality principle, which operates in opposition to the pleasure principle, is not a mental reflection of a universal social condition; rather, it is a reflection of historicity, of concrete socioeconomic, political, and historical restrictions that function as barriers against the attainment of pleasure and self-fulfillment. These barriers forced Kierkegaard into the adoption and philosophical formulation of the subjective absolute, which is the ultimate reflection, in 19th century class society, of the recollection of a pre-historic or trans-historic happiness. For Kierkegaard, the concept of <u>gentagelse</u>, transcendental continuity, served a profoundly therapeutic, epistemological, and perhaps even political role, because, through the understanding of this concept, the individual could become liberated from his state of demonic unfreedom and from his fear of self-revelation.

The type of memory that is attached to the past is a negative, non-revolutionary memory that does not externalize, i.e., express socially and politically, the internal energies of freedom and desire. I saw this type of memory as an obstruction to individual and social change in <u>A Portrait</u>, <u>Ulysses</u>, and <u>Havoc</u>. These novels represent, I believe, a diversion of revolutionary energy into wish-fulfillments and imaginary satisfactions; they represent a regression into the demonic state of fixation, symbolized, for example, by the fish in <u>Havoc</u>. The works of Sigmund Freud take a dualistic approach that partly validates his own theory of regression, the principle of repetition, or, the biological concept of a return to an inorganic state. The biological determinism inherent in Freud's works creates, by itself, the idea of a death instinct, an instinct that manifested itself in *Ulysses* and *Havoc*; both novels represented a descent into a kind of memory from which there was no return. This type of regressive - and repressive - memory succumbs to the reality principle, as the human consciousness, or rather, the idology on which consciousness is based, confuses a social condition with a universal, metaphysical absolute. The necessary state of unfreedom is accepted as people live in what Stephen Dedalus called the nightmare of the past. Freud's reality principle was defined as a psychic instrument by which the individual could adapt to external necessity; but external necessity is socioeconomic, historical. Reality is a socio-historical organization that affects the mental structure through specific societal agencies. Freud's theory, then, generalizes from a specific historical form of reality to reality itself. Naturally, all historical forms are based on a partly repressive organization of the instincts, as societal repression is infused into the psyche, and civilization itself has progressed as organized domination. This organized domination assumes the guise of a universal biological determinism for Freud and is responsible for the metapsychological idea of a death instinct as being operative in all civilization; the principle of organized domination is also responsible for Kierkegaard's demonic category.

Marcuse extrapolates from Freud's theory by a duplication of concepts, by coupling the biological and sociohistorical concepts. He arrives at two new terms: "surplus-repression", i.e. the restrictions necessitated by social domination, as distinguished from repression, i.e., the instinctual modifications necessary for the perpetuation of the human race; and "performance principle", i.e. the local historical form of the reality principle.[1] Because of sociohistorical phenomena such as disease, poverty, oppression of entire social classes, and repression of sexuality, the cultural power of Eros is obstructed, is prevented from achieving its objective, namely the creation of constructive communal ties and relationships. The performance principle which governs the specific historical form we call Capitalism, stratifies society according to the competitive economic performances of its members. Freud basically turned "competition" into "aggressiveness" and into the "death instinct", seeing these negative forces as being mollified only through sublimation; he did not re-think the culture he lived in, but posited an eternal ahistorical conflict between sexuality and civilization. The regression of sexuality and its subsequent transformation into aggression is, however, achieved through social domination, contrived to preserve the prevailing class structure:

> The organization of sexuality reflects the basic features of the performance principle and its organization of society. Freud emphasizes the aspect of centralization. It is especially operative in the "unification" of the various objects of the partial instincts into one libidinal object of the opposite sex, and in the establishment of genital supremacy. In both cases, the unifying process is repressive - that is to say, the partial instincts do not develop freely into a "higher" state of gratification which preserves their objectives, but are cut off and reduced to subservient functions. This process achieves the socially necessary desexualization of the body: the libido becomes concentrated in one part of the body, leaving most of the rest free for use as the instrument of labor. The temporal reduction of the libido is thus supplemented by its spatial reduction.[2]

A state of elevated, almost euphoric sexuality was achieved in *Hunger* as the poetic subject *experienced* a reunion with the woman of his dreams, dreams whose imagery recalled the early, pre-Oedipal stage of fusion with the maternal Eros; in *A Portrait*, *Ulysses*, and *Havoc*, sexuality remained fragmented, also on the subliminal level of dream consciousness. The poetic subjects, or protagonists, of these novels rebelled against any form of reintegration and thus became alienated from themselves, as well as from society. I see this rebellion as a result of the infusion into the psyche of social domination; the infusion penetrates and pervades the mind of the poetic subject even to the extent that he cannot separate external reality from his own internal longings and pursuits. In this manner, the division of labor exploits and divides not only social classes, but also the individual mind, and the attempt made by literary art to create wholeness and harmony becomes aborted and thwarted. The division of the mind reaches into the most private, intimate corners of the soul, influencing sexual feeling and sexual behavior, with devastating results in regard to the male protagonist's relationship to women. Ulysses and Havoc represent and describe the "socially necessary desexualization of the body". I have described the rebellion of Kierkegaard's demonic personality as a kind of re-sexualization, but we might just as well apply Marcuse's phrase to it and designate it as " desexualization of the body", since the rebellion is the thwarted, partly masochistic response of the ego to the domination and punishment perpetrated by the super-ego. The demonic personality is engaged in an impotent form of rebellion, as he is ejected from Eternity into Temporality, thus becoming subject to time and its existential limitations. The protagonists of <u>Ulysses</u> and <u>Havoc</u> were subjugated to time and history, although they exhibited a desperate attempt to overcome social and sexual alienation by creating a new "form of the soul", and by experimenting with the idea of an androgynous type, a sexually liberated and undifferentiated individual who would be able to transcend the division of labor.

The actual, unrepressed form of Eros, however, is liberation from time, as "timelessness is the ideal of pleasure".[3] If the human instincts were to attain fulfillment in a non-repressive social order, Freud's "compulsion to repeat" would lose its biological rationale, and Eros would be liberated from time, appearing as a concrete Utopia.

> To be sure, the threat of time, the passing of the moment of fullness, the anxiety over the end, may themselves become erotogenic - obstacles that "swell the tide of the libido." However, the wish of Faust which conjures the pleasure principle demands, not the beautiful moment but eternity. With its striving for eternity, Eros offends against the decisive taboo that sanctions libidinal pleasure only as a temporal and controlled condition, not as a permanent fountainhead of the human existence. Indeed, if the alliance between time and the established order dissolved, "natural" private unhappiness would no longer support organized societal unhappiness. The relegation of human fulfillment to utopia would no longer find adequate response in the instincts of man, and the drive for liberation would assume that terrifying force which actually it never had.[4]

The drive towards liberation is at the core of the hermeneutic activity which manifests itself, in art and politics, as a reunion of instinct and reason; Eros, as the life instinct, imbues the individual and his culture with an unconscious desire to transcend the continuum of history, and reason elevates that desire to a conscious wish, a wish to create a new societal form that has been instinctually grasped and intellectually formulated through recollection, i.e., gentagelse of the temps perdu, not as idealization of the past, but as a re-constituted present and future time in man's history. Kierkegaard's view of time substantiates this integration of instinct and reason, since spirit, ånd, is posited as the fusion of the physical and the intellectual. The positing of the spirit is the creation of the moment, øjeblikket, the intersection of the eternal and the temporal; or, as Kierkegaard puts it, øjeblikket is the incognito of Eternity, its appearance in time. Eternity will appear behind the present as time past, as it happened in Ulysses and Havoc, if the moment is not constituted as the present and future projection of Eternity, i.e., of the timelessness that is the "ideal of pleasure". In øjeblikket, the future manifests itself as the re-projected past; the past, as instinct and desire, is consciously reflected and re-formulated in

Kierkegaard's ethical and religious categories. Past instinct becomes present and future reason, a revolutionary mode of reason that transcends current history. In Marxian terms, current history is only the <u>appearance</u> of phenomena; revolutionary reason creates, through dialectical insight, new societal forms that express the true <u>essence</u> of phenomena; true essence contains and liberates the human need for self-fulfillment, and the essence of phenomena produces a new ideology.

Kierkegaard achieves self-fulfillment, not via political ideology but via theological speculation and faith; his emphasis on the subjective absolute, however, indicates that he possessed a revolutionary energy that is the equivalent of Marcuse's utopian impulse, although Kierkegaard's energy did not become politically channelized.

The concept of <u>Øjeblikket</u> is an important part of Kierkegaard's definition of "being" and "non-being", essence and appearance. The moment can be "the momentary", i.e., related to temporal existence as sensuality, as it is in aesthetic enjoyment; or, the moment can reveal essence in its relation to eternal being. The moment as sensuality, as pure aesthetic enjoyment, is superficial and expresses the predominant aspect of time: its fleeting nature and its fragmentation, the mechanical succession of past, present, and future. This mechanical aspect of time does, of course, reflect the socioeconomic organization that divides the human psyche, human labor, and human time into fractions, thus producing a devaluation of the human dimension of wholeness, and preventing this dimension from erupting into history as a fully unfolded future re-projection of the past or prehistoric happiness. Mechanical time is therefore not historical time, because it merely creates the appearance of a dialectical process. The dialectical evolution of societal forms is achieved through the fusion of past, present, and future into spirit, ånd, or essence. The essence of humanity, or human-ness is suppressed under Capitalism, and it becomes the purpose and function of art and philosophy to reproduce that suppressed reality by negating that which is. For Kierkegaard, that negation produced the subjective absolute that is related to Øjeblikket, the timelessness of desire, the "fullness of time" - tidens fylde:

> On the whole, in defining the concepts of the past, the future, and the eternal, it can be seen how the moment is defined. If there is no moment, the eternal appears behind as the past. It is as when I imagine a man walking along a road but do not posit the step, and so the road appears behind him as the distance covered. If the moment is posited but merely as a discrimen (division), then the future is the eternal. If the moment is

> posited, so is the eternal, but also the future,
> which reappears as the past. This is clearly seen
> in the Greek, the Jewish, and the Christian views.
> The pivotal concept in Christianity, that which
> made all things new, is the fullness of time, but
> the fullness of time is the moment as the eternal,
> and yet this eternal is also the future and the
> past. If attention is not paid to this, not a
> single concept can be saved from a heretical
> and treasonable admixture that annihilates the
> concept. One does not get the past by itself
> but in a simple continuity with the future (with
> this the concepts of conversion, atonement, and
> redemption are lost in the world-historical sig-
> nificance and lost in the individual historical
> development). The future is not by itself but in
> a simple continuity with the present (thereby the
> concepts of resurrection and judgment are destroyed).[5]

Eternity enters time, that is, as future <u>gentagelse</u>, continuity and evolution of the past, rather than mere repetition of the past. Kierkegaard's concept of time thus parallels the hermeneutical superposition of perception: the superposition of eternal being upon temporal being. Remaining in the temporal and the purely sensual reveals a fear of true freedom, a fear of undertaking the qualitative leap into freedom, <u>det qualitative Spring</u>.[6] The possibility of freedom and of an actualized, real future produces <u>angst</u>, the symptom of <u>syndighed</u>, sinfulness, which, deprived of its theological or moral connotation, simply denotes the state of being in time rather than being in Eternity. If we equate "Eternity" with future history, or future time, with a societal form that can contain and promote human happiness and fulfillment, then Kierkegaard's impetus towards freedom becomes equivalent to the utopian impulse, and the Danish philosopher becomes a revolutionary thinker with some political potential.

William Faulkner's novels are full of characters who are trapped by mechanical time. Quentin's clock that belonged to his father and grandfather is called "the mausoleum of all hope and desire",[7] the watch tells "its furious lie on the dark table" as Quentin longs to be suspended from time:

> A quarter hour yet. And then I'll not be. The peacefullest words. Peacefullest words. *Non fui. Sum. Fui. Nom sum.* Somewhere I heard bells once. Mississippi or Massachusetts. I was. I am not. Massachusetts or Mississippi. Shreve has a bottle in his trunk. *Aren't you even going to open it* Mr and Mrs Jason Richmond Compson announce the *Three times. Days. Aren't you even going to open it* marriage of their daughter Candace *that liquor teaches you to confuse the means with the end.* I am. Drink. I was not.[8]

Quentin's relationship to timelessness is problematic, first of all because it involves death, complete non-being, as the ultimate suspension from time; the "peacefullest words" are the words "then I'll not be"; Quentin's longing for real being is, paradoxically, a longing for death. Secondly, his relationship to timelessness, to what has been referred to as "the ideal of pleasure", is problematic because it presents us with a seemingly paradoxical juxtaposition of reason and emotion. Quentin's longing is highly emotional; it is a passionate longing for death. Yet his longing is expressed rationally - it becomes a logical thought process measured <u>in time</u>. As Quentin puts it: "<u>A quarter hour yet. And then I'll not be</u>" [emphasis mine]. Quentin tries to attain timelessness through time, through a measured, intellectual process that reflects the temporal aspect of existence. Quentin will not be <u>in a quarter hour</u>. It is obvious that, on a deeper level, Faulkner describes the existential struggle of his protagonists to create future being; this future state of being becomes synonymous with death at this point because Quentin tries to solve the problem of being by means of logical discourse. But his discourse is suffused with passion, manifested most strongly in the phrase "the peacefullest words". This passionate longing points to a future being, and it could create a new form of being.

    A similar thought process is presented in one of Darl's monologues in <u>As I Lay Dying</u> (1930):

> In a strange room you must empty yourself for sleep. And before you are emptied for sleep, what are you. And when you are emptied for sleep, you are not. And when you are filled

> with sleep, you never were. I dont know what
> I am. I dont know if I am or not. Jewel
> knows he is, because he does not know that
> he does not know whether he is or not. He
> cannot empty himself for sleep because he is
> not what he is and he is what he is not.
> Beyond the unlamped wall I can hear the rain
> shaping the wagon that is ours, the load that
> is no longer theirs that felled and sawed it
> nor yet theirs that bought it and which is
> not ours either, lie on our wagon though it
> does, since only the wind and the rain shape
> it only to Jewel and me, that are not asleep.
> And since sleep is is-not and rain and wind
> are *was*, it is not. Yet the wagon *is*, because
> when the wagon is *was*, Addie Bundren will not
> be. And Jewel *is*, so Addie Bundren must be.
> And then I must be, or I could not empty
> myself for sleep in a strange room. And so
> if I am not emptied yet, I am *is*.
>
> How often have I lain beneath rain on a
> strange roof, thinking of home.[9]

Darl's reasoning is a logical attempt to define being objectively; more specifically, his being, and the wagon's being. Darl juggles the tenses, past, present, and future, in the phrase: "the wagon is, because when the wagon is was, Addie Bundren will not be", and his reasoning works from a theoretical point of view. Present being is determined by past and future being, and Darl's reasoning is an example of Kierkegaard's "remembering forward". Darl's whole being is determined by his ability to see what is going to happen in the future, or what is happening somewhere else. He is not merely clairvoyant; he thinks ahead, in the Kierkegaardian sense of experiencing eternity as

the future within the present. The moment of Darl's
"is-ness" is the moment of eternal being, øjeblikket,
which Kierkegaard describes as follows:

> "The moment" is a figurative expression, and
> therefore it is not easy to deal with. However,
> it is a beautiful word to consider. Nothing is
> as swift as a blink of the eye, and yet it is
> commensurable with the concept of the eternal.
> Thus when Ingeborg looks out over the sea
> after Frithiof, this is a picture of what is
> expressed in the figurative word. An outburst of
> her emotion, a sigh or a word, already has as a
> sound more of the determination of time and is
> more present as something that is vanishing and
> does not have in it so much of the presence of the
> eternal. For this reason a sigh, a word, etc. have
> power to relieve the soul of the burdensome weight,
> precisely because the burden, when merely expressed,
> already begins to become something of the past. A
> blink is therefore a designation of time, but mark
> well, of time in the fateful conflict when it is
> touched by eternity. 10

Darl is present, nærværende, in the sense, at
least, that he reasons correctly. Yet the passage ends
with the curious phrase: "How often have I lain beneath
rain on a strange roof, thinking of home." The line
expresses longing, alienation, and homelessness; the
natural elements, the wind and rain, shape a being that
does not coincide or coexist with Darl's own being,
although he sees how the rain shapes the wagon; that
which Darl is not is his "home", his quintessential
spiritual being. He has defined present existence and

has glimpsed øjeblikket,[11] eternity in the moment.

But Darl is away from home, and, as in Quentin's case, home could be death, non-being; that hypothesis is academic, however. It is far more important to point out that Darl is a vehicle for, a mediator of, the future state of being that we have called Eros, the timeless dimension of existence. Darl attempts to fuse with the cultural Matrix through the process of remembering forward; hence his attempt to get rid of the dead mother and the coffin that the other family members want to preserve.

Darl's attempt to burn the coffin places him in stark contrast to his brother Jewel who is bent on completing the journey to town. Jewel is strongly tied to his mother even after death. The Mother Image assumes its negative aspect here, turning into the evil, engulfing counterpart to the symbol of culture and creativity. The negative presentation of the mother image is a result of Jewel's subjective fantasies about his mother, fantasies which reveal a strong passion for the mother, and which finally make him create a substitute, the horse. Addie Bundren herself does not promote or endorse dependency in any way, searching, on the contrary, for the freedom that resides in action, as opposed to the imprisonment and falsehood of words.

Anse, her husband, is a user and abuser of words:

> So I took Anse. And when I knew that I had Cash, I knew that living was terrible and that this was the answer to it. That was when I learned that words are no good; that words dont ever fit even what they are trying to say at. When he was born I knew that motherhood was invented by someone who had to have a word for it because the ones that had the children didn't care whether there was a word for it or not. I knew that fear was invented by someone that had never had the fear; pride, who never had the pride. I knew that it had been, not that they had dirty noses, but that we had had to use one another by words like spiders dangling by their mouths from a beam, swinging and twisting and never touching, and that only through the blows of the switch could my blood and their blood flow as one stream. I knew that it had been, not that my aloneness had to be violated over and over each day, but that it had never been violated until Cash came. Not even by Anse in the nights.
>
> He had a word, too. Love, he called it. But I had been used to words for a long time. I knew that that word was like the others: just a shape to fill a lack; that when the right time came, you wouldn't need a word for that anymore than for pride or fear. Cash did not need to say it to me nor I to him, and I would say, Let Anse use it, if he wants to. So that it was Anse or love; love or Anse: it didn't matter.[12]

Addie's children are of her alone, "of the wild blood boiling along the earth".[13] Darl is her second-born and reiterates her proclivity towards unrelenting truthfulness; he also echoes her creative, poetic language. Darl knows how "our lives ravel out into the no-wind, no-sound, the weary gestures wearily recapitulant";[14] he shares with her the intimate knowledge of the "dark voicelessness in which the words are the deeds".[15] Darl's words <u>are</u> deeds, in the sense that they look through, even predict, the intimate acts of other people. His sister Dewey Dell, for one, is aware of his ability to see into people's minds:

> The land runs out of Darl's eyes; they swim to pinpoints. They begin at my feet and rise along my body to my face, and then my dress is gone: I sit naked on the seat above the unhurrying mules, above the travail.[16]

"The land runs out of Darl's eyes." This phrase emphasizes the point that Darl is poised between and communicates with two worlds: the temporal and the eternal one; he possesses being in the "glance of his eyes", <u>øjeblikket</u>, in which one knows the reality of being, and in which being becomes identical with action. The ambivalence of Darl's being is most poignantly revealed in his conversation with Vardaman:

> "Jewel's mother is a horse," Darl said.
> "Then mine can be a fish, cant it, Darl? I said.
> Jewel is my brother.
> "Then mine will have to be a horse, too," I said.
> "Why?" Darl Said. "If pa is your pa, why does your ma have to be a horse just because Jewel's is?"
> "Why does it?" I said. "Why does it, Darl?"
> Darl is my brother.

> "Then what is your ma, Darl?" I said.
> "I haven't got ere one," Darl said. "Because if I had one, it is *was*. And if it is was, it cant be *is*. Can it."
> "No," I said.
> "Then I am not," Darl said. "Am I?"
> "No," I said.
> I am, Darl is my brother.
> "But you *are*, Darl," I said.
> "I know it," Darl said. "That's why I am not *is*. *Are* is too many for one woman to foal."[17]

Darl is <u>are</u>; his logical definition of his mother's being is irrefutable: she is <u>was</u>, therefore not is. Claiming that she still exists would mean falsifying being. Darl remains true to her memory in the sense that he represents, like her, a negation of false being, of non-being. In consequence of his own logic, then, he represents being and future being as liberation from the past. The nature and character that he shares with Quentin, however, precipitates him into a tragic discrepancy between logic and emotion, and he ends up being divided from himself, talking about himself in the third person as he is sent to the asylum:

> Darl is our brother, our brother Darl. Our brother Darl in a cage in Jackson where, his grimed hands lying light in the quiet interstices, looking out he foams.
> "Yes yes yes yes yes yes yes yes."[18]

Darl's consciousness of time itself contributes to his internal division; but he passionately wants the action of the novel to evolve into future time, symbolized by the road, and he does experience future time through the ability to see into the future. He is held back from becoming what he is by his family's insistence upon paying tribute to the dead mother and their insisting on remaining in the past.

The river that they have to cross with the loaded wagon becomes symbolic, as experienced by Darl, of the ambivalent nature of time: history as past time, desolation, futility; and future time as creative action. Darl recognizes the dual aspect of time, time as the life and the death that are left as imprints on Nature itself:

> The river itself is not a hundred yards across, and pa and Vernon and Vardaman and Dewey Dell are the only things in sight not of that single monotony of desolation leaning with that terrific quality a little from right to left, as though we had reached the place where the motion of the wasted world accelerates just before the final precipice. Yet they appear dwarfed. It is as though the space between us were time: an irrevocable quality. It is as though time, no longer running straight before us in a diminishing line, now runs parallel between us like a looping string, the distance being the doubling accretion of the thread and not the interval between.[19]

The "irrevocable quality" of time stands between Darl and the rest of the family; the river can conduct them on, or it can reduce them to slaves of their own past. Darl wants to instigate action and change; this is what separates him from the other family members, as Addie Bundren was separated from them. Darl and his family are physically close, yet divided from one another by an immense temporal space which is described as "the doubling accretion of the thread and not the interval between".

Darl does not reach his "home", does not attain full being, but is, nonetheless, suspended between time and eternity, between necessity and freedom, and this suspense creates insanity in the end; his insanity is the result of the absurdity and pain of clearly seeing, envisioning, and to an extent <u>experiencing</u> absolute being and freedom as liberation from the past. Darl possesses a human dimension. I define this dimension as the integration, in this case the temporary integration, of the temporal and the eternal which includes a complete identity between the spatial and the temporal; this identity is the sign of "divine" being. Time approximates future time in Darl's consciousness; he "remembers forward". Addie is <u>was</u> for Darl, but he becomes her future - her truth is projected into the future by him, so that there is a significant integration between Faulkner's protagonist and the maternal Eros, the creative Matrix. In Darl, there is no real separation between "having been" and "becoming"; he is present, nærværende, in time and space, as he defines time as the "doubling accretion of the thread and not the interval between". This is time defined in spatial terms, not only logically, abstractly deduced, but perceived poetically and experienced emotionally.

The passage quoted expresses the closest possible approximation to real being, to the simultaneity of the nacheinander (time) and the nebeneinander (space) that Stephen Dedalus divided from one another in Ulysses due to the abstract and purely intellectual nature of his thought and his being. Stephen and Darl are both logical thinkers, sophists, but Darl cancels or annuls the non-being, the deceit, of pure sophistry as he experiences being as becoming. Non-being turns into its own opposite, paradoxically; the process of negation turns into a process of affirmation.

The negating function that produces its own opposite is the central principle behind Pär Lagerkvist's novel The Dwarf (1945). The dwarf, the narrator and protagonist of the novel, initially represents a negation of the human dimension; yet the narrative gradually achieves an affirmation of human values. The dwarf's first-person narrative, which occurs in a Renaissance setting, the court of a Machiavellian Prince, slowly changes its perspective vis a vis the dwarf's two most significant opponents: the artist Bernardo and the Princess, both of whom he does not understand in the beginning; the dwarf says of the Princess:

> Her face is not at all interesting. It is easy to see that she is a harlot, though she hides it beneath a smooth deceitful surface. It does not need much observation to realize that. And then what is there left to study and seek after in her lascivious face? What fascination does it hold?
> But he is obviously fascinated by everything. I have seen him pick up a stone from the ground and examine it with the deepest interest, turn and twist it, and finally pocket it, as though it were a rarity. Anything and everything seems to fascinate him. Is he a lunatic?
> An enviable lunatic! One for whom a pebble has value must be surrounded by treasures wherever he goes. 20

The dwarf's gradual understanding of the Princess' significance for him as a man and as a human being is linked to the artistic work of Maestro Bernardo, for it is through his painting of the Princess that the dwarf's perception of reality itself is changed. The narrator's attitude to Bernardo is negative, initially:

> Messer Bernado's meddlings and his inquisitive interest in everything are repugnant to me. What is the use of it all? What sensible object does it serve? It repels me to think that he should have in his possession a portrait of me, that he

> should own me in this way. It is as though I
> were no longer sole owner of myself, as though
> I were also over there in Santa Croce, among
> his detestable monsters. 21

The reference to Bernardo's freakish images, the misshapen monsters of the painter's mind, becomes the first indication that the dwarf has begun thinking about another existential dimension; he usually expresses a cynical rationality, a lucid, but reductive sophistication that makes him doubt all things human, and he thinks of himself as belonging to another race, a race that hates humanity. It is revealed through his own words, though, that his hatred is due to maternal deprivation, and the dialectic of the narrative focuses on the slow unfolding of the dwarf's own _human_ personality, which has remained subconscious throughout the major part of his life. From the dwarf's point of view, the human mind is equivocal, and he searches for simplicity and clarity. The human psyche has a subliminal sphere that the narrator has not been exposed to prior to the meeting with the artist (the model for whom, obviously, is the Renaissance genius, Leonardo da Vinci). The dwarf's own subconscious manifests itself in a dream about the Maestro:

> Last night I had a horrible dream. I thought that
> I saw Maestro Bernado standing on a high mountain,

> tall and imposing with his gray hair and his
> mighty brow, but the air about his head was full
> of monsters flapping on bats' wings, all the
> foul freaks which I knew from his drawings in
> Santa Croce. They fluttered about him like imps
> and it seemed as though he were their master.
> Their ghostly faces resembled those of lizards and
> toads, but his remained grave, stern and noble.
> He seemed just the same as usual. Then, by slow
> degrees, his body underwent a change. It became
> shrunken and misshapen, and crumpled wings
> sprouted forth which joined to the thin hairy
> legs like those of a bat. His face was as solemn
> as before, but he began to flutter his wings
> and suddenly he rose and flew away with the other
> gruesome creatures into the darkness of the night.
>   I do not bother about dreams; they mean nothing
> and make no difference. Reality is the only
> thing that matters.
>   Obviously he must be misshapen; I decided
> that long ago. 22

In this dream, he sees Bernardo changing shape and becoming like the monsters of his paintings, paintings that also contain a paradoxical beauty, and the narrator has to concede to the fact that beauty and ugliness may coexist. He rejects this proposition initially, but his understanding of it evolves further during the narrative, and it culminates in the last part of the narrative, at the point where the Maestro has completed the portrait of the Princess, who exemplifies beauty and ugliness in one. The dwarf admits that she is the only one he *could* love, if indeed he were capable of loving someone belonging to the alien human race:

> I can quite understand why the Prince loves her. Not that I ever could myself, but that is quite different. Could I ever really love anybody? I do not know. If I could love, it would have been the Princess. But now I hate her instead.
> And yet I do feel that she is the only one whom I could ever have loved. Why that should be is quite beyond me. I do not understand it at all.
> Truly love is something of which one knows nothing. 23

Later, the dwarf admits openly to the Princess herself that he has suffered for her - it has been painful for him to see her receive her lovers. With this concession, the dwarf reveals his human dimension in spite of himself.

The dwarf can be said to epitomize the demonic, the Satanic, an inversion of Christ, and the negation of all human values, since his actions are mainly motivated by hatred. He conducts, for example, a black mass in the court, and he is responsible for the murder of the Princess' chief lover. These acts, however, are only a prelude to a distorted, painful act of self-revelation through which the demonic personality, as Kierkegaard describes it, is propelled towards freedom in spite of itself. The narrator is imprisoned in his own mind, and his imprisonment, his limitation, can be derived from human psychology; the dwarf can be interpreted as a repressive type who denies his own human qualities, but yet must give in to them. The revelation of the narrator's alter ego is instigated by art and love, the cultural Eros that creates future life in spite of the historically "necessary" limitations, the restrictions of time that the narrator has been subject to. It is not incidental that the narrative takes place in the Renaissance; the socioeconomic organization and structure of feudal society forms an external correspondence to the repressive, and repressed, psychological type. The stratified class structure of the feudal state becomes a social, historical extension of the imprisoned, stratified mind. This mind does, however, achieve liberation to the extent that it perceives a potentially free dimension of existence; it is the author's intended irony that the narrator recognizes this freedom, this liberated Eros, but yet rejects and negates it on one level of the narrative itself. The first-person narrative, which expresses the dwarf's own perspective on the surface, is thus deceptive since the dwarf subjects himself to irony and expresses a totally different perspective on another level of the narrative, a perspective that is inherent in and emanates from his own character, his own "subconscious". The dwarf's demonic, unfree existence, his non-being that is characterized by self-deception, evolves into being, and the narrator reveals himself as a human being. The restrictions of time and history are removed as Eros erupts within the human consciousness.

In spite of the reductive perspective of the first-person narrative, the "I" of the novel becomes the mediator of a more constructive point of view, especially if we agree that the cosmos of the novel is the creation of the narrator. What has been enclosed in itself, indesluttet, reveals itself in spite of itself and reprojects an image of human freedom. The dwarf becomes symbolic of the duality of freedom and imprisonment in the modern world as Lagerkvist sees it. The social outcast who is an integral part of modern political reality achieves an approximation to freedom and Eros through catharsis; affirmation is produced by negation.

Martin A. Hansen's novel The Liar (1950) is a first-person narrative like Lagerkvist's The Dwarf and the internal conflict is one between negation and affirmation, between deception and truth, between logical analysis and passionate experience. The narrator, Johannes Vig is a schoolteacher living on an isolated island; he moved there from the mainland in order to create meaning in his life and in order to escape from the past, a past that had become his Fate, an inescapable internal reality. Johannes, the "liar", is a seeker of truth who tries to peel off the layers of deceit through the process of narration. His internal reality has consisted of a pattern of destructive sexual emotions, a pattern which he is now trying to break. In a conversation with one of his former students, Annemari whom he loves (so he tells us), Johannes admits to his own deceitful behavior and reveals the actual motivation behind his actions:

> You must bear with me, Annemari, for making up a story last night.
> She is looking at me in the mirror, and she smiles, but her smile is fading.
> I had to make moral tales, those were my conditions, I'm saying, and didn't I tell you about a certain Birte? Yes, she was my loved one at one time, and then a friend took her away. Later I met them again. And I told you how I withdrew virtuously and left so that nothing would happen between her and me. A fine story.
> Well, what did you really do?
> You didn't have to reproach me with not obeying the law of love, or whatever it's called. I did that thoroughly. He had taken her from me. All right, I came back and had my revenge.
> Then is it true what you are telling me now, Johannes?
> You can always believe in the evil things I tell you, my girl. (J.V.) 24

Johannes has experienced repeated difficulties with triangular relationships, losing a woman to another man, or "stealing" a woman from someone else in order to get revenge for the previous loss; his escape from his former self has succeeded only partially, because he repeats the compulsive behavior of his past, attempting to take Annemari from Oluf, another student, and indirectly causing the death of Oluf's brother, Niels, in a boating accident. Johannes reveals to the reader, the honest and gullible Natanael, that he wished for Oluf's death in that accident, and that he could have prevented the two men from going out to sea. The narrator typifies the Freudian "compulsion to repeat", and he has to admit that he is what he is, irrevocably:

> I can say "yesyes" or "nono", but whatever else a person like me says is actually deceiving. "Yesyes" or "nono". The chase is over, but the dream is also extinguished. Yes, I can choose my fate, and I can fight, but I cannot grow. I cannot make myself over, I know that. Only the Great Moulder can remould a person if He wants to. My weakness and my sin is great, for I only know that God is near when He hits me hard. (J.V.) 25

Johannes reveals another Freudian feature: the sense of guilt that is derived from a punitive superego, called God by the narrator. This God is a distinctly Old Testament God:

> Yes, it has even come to this, when the night forebodes my future loneliness, where I must be alone with what I know and alone with a mighty

> Scourger, that I have turned against Him like
> a Job, growling in my pain, like someone who
> would rather be cut down in a brief, violent
> struggle than suffer the burning wound of
> privation. (J.V.) 26

His moral sense is produced by sexual renunciation, a manifestation of a masochistic ego, as Freud describes it in <u>Civilization and Its Discontents</u>. Yet Johannes gradually realizes and experiences a new moral sentiment in himself, and a new vocation in life, a change that is made possible only by the renunciation of past behavior patterns.

> Down below was the island, like the giant body
> of a monster. And I did not imagine, as one often
> does, that I understood it deep down. It was a
> monster that would swallow human beings and
> devour generations so that all would be forgotten.
> Granted, in the daylight it assumes a shape we
> are familiar with. But it has only acquired this
> shape by being vanquished by the mind, tied down
> by language, and by being conquered by the culture
> that we doubt too much. That is my belief. Every
> generation must conquer the island. Conquering it
> is an achievement of the human spirit. Borrowing
> its beauty is merely parasitic and has nothing to
> do with spirit. Spirit means ploughing the earth,
> putting pen to paper in order to win the island
> through knowledge. (J.V.) 27

He believes he can conquer the island through scientific knowledge. This insight on part of the narrator is an expression of Martin A. Hansen's own changing values, his value judgment on literary fiction in general and on the function of art in society. The author came to see fiction as <u>deceit</u>, and came to realize the importance of objective description; the narrator's growing understanding of his own personal life is conducive of a gradual approximation to this authorial viewpoint, the author's skepticism towards art itself. The author's viewpoint, then, creates the moral and cognitive norm of the novel, and this norm is revealed as the narrator reveals himself through a web of lies and irony. Johannes changes from an aesthete, from a Kierkegaardian seducer, into a more mature person who rejects the aesthetic point of view; as in Kierkegaard's novel <u>Diary of a Seducer</u>, the seducer becomes a mediator of love, an instigator of a new emotion in a woman, and as in Kierkegaard's work, the seducer also becomes a mediator of a new self through self-doubt and self-irony. The esthete looks ahead; he is dialectically connected with the future as another dimension of his own self, and thus he ultimately negates his own negation. It is my opinion that both Kierkegaard's and Martin A. Hansen's works must be interpreted from such a dialectical point of view; if we preclude this point of view, we overlook the dynamic aspect of their existential philosophy.

Johannes' experience of himself as a seducer also becomes an intense experience of alienation and despair.

The experience occurs in a central passage of the novel, where he is giving a sermon at the island church (he functions as substitute preacher):

> A suspicion creeps into my mind, cold like an eel, but it does not disturb my calm. You are possessed. A stranger, an alien force more powerful than you filled up the void of your soul as you got up from your seat. You are possessed. Loki is standing here now. The eyes of Loki hold them in a spell. It is a demonic deception.
> Yes, if they came to see me, wanting to discuss the existence of Evil with me, I would have made light of it. Yes, I would make light of it.
> Maybe the pride of my own vacant mind, the pride of nothingness itself, has unexpectedly turned into a lust for power. I do not know. But it is as if a mighty, cunning Spirit inhabits me. He makes me much stronger as a man. His mouth curls in a smooth, seductive smile. The people sitting down there have no will of their own any more. Look at the women, they are spellbound. Oluf's mother, Rigmor, Annemari. On the organ bench she sits, devoid of will. (J.V.) 28

Johannes' seductive smile is reduced to the "pride of nothingness", <u>Intethedens Hovmod</u>. He recognizes his own hubris, his emptiness, as he compares himself to the unclean spirit that is exorcised by Christ:

> Maybe I was tempted to say something, dangerously tempted. But what could I truly say about words like these: when the unclean Spirit is excorcised from a human soul, he will roam through barren places, seeking rest; and when he does not find it, he says: "I will return to the house I left." What do you think of those words? Do you think the island vicar can even touch such a strange and wild image. The unclean Spirit is exiled, banished from his human

> habitation, dragging his legs through arid deserts,
> finding nothing to drink, not a dew drop, nor a
> green blade of grass. Did you imagine the Evil Spirit
> to be a suffering spirit, Nathanael?
> Well, then the desperate unclean Spirit remembers
> his home, and he returns to it. And when he enters
> his house, he finds it swept and cleaned. Then he
> leaves and seeks out seven more Spirits worse than
> himself, and they all come back to live there; and
> the end of this human being will be worse than his
> beginning. (J.V.) 29

The "unclean spirit" is the person who is divided against himself. Christ symbolizes wholeness, integration, and the coming of Christ, which is synonymous with a radical inner change, is signalled by the arrival of the bird of spring, the snipe. The snipe also symbolizes love, eroticism, in its pure, unquestioning form, and the fact that Johannes hunts the bird and finds it may indicate that his self-doubt and his irony have paved the way to an understanding of his role as a mediator: he has become a "seducer", in the significant sense that he creates change in another individual; he creates love in Rigmor, and he himself experiences this change, if not in himself, then at least through the woman who accompanies him on his bird hunt.

The snipe's habitat is described as a "wild undergrowth":

> The birch woods are not forested, the farms have had plots there for many generations; during the war some trees were felled, but haphazardly so. There is a wild and widespread undergrowth of creeping plants, bushes, small trees, and above it tower some very crooked trees with intertwining branches, covered with fungi and excrescences. The birch forest is in some places labyrinthine, growing wild, and is enchanting to the wanderer. (J.V.) 30

The habitat is part of the natural forest and has not been cut or cultivated by humans. The imagery of this symbolic passage reflects the natural human element, the pure life that must be extracted from its state of repression. The extraction of subconscious material from the "undergrowth" forms the psychological action of the novel; unconscious material is made conscious, deceit becomes truth, and the liar is lifted into self-awareness.

The hermeneutical process of the text is clothed in a religious language. I interpret the religious overtone in the novel as a language that clarifies Johannes' experience, not as a reference to a higher reality. However, a higher reality is present in the text as Johannes' ideal of himself, an ideality that he cannot reach in himself. He must resign himself to the role of mediator, a "guest on earth"; but the psychological, internal action of the text re-projects and reaffirms Eros by unveiling past time and by transcending it. Johannes' final realization is that he loved Rigmor, not Annemari:

> I have not seen her since the snipe hunt. I could go over there now and take her, bring her home to my house. It would never work. I would soon stifle the life that grows in her. I know that. I almost stifled it once before. She was the one I really cared for, but I deceived myself and others, pretending it was someone else. I enjoyed that game. But I know she will grow, that her spirit will be fertile and thriving. She is different from me, and I could only help her that one time. And now we will not talk about that any more, Nathanael. (J.V.) [31]

Johannes was the cause of the love experienced by Rigmor, and he resigns himself to letting it grow without interfering, without taking what is "rightfully" his. The narrator's personality has undergone an absolute change as deception has turned into truth, non-being into being.

CHAPTER V REFERENCES

[1] Herbert Marcuse, *Eros and Civilization* (Boston: Beacon Press, 1966), p. 35 ff.

[2] Marcuse, p. 48.

[3] Marcuse, p. 231.

[4] Marcuse, p. 234.

[5] Søren Kierkegaard, *The Concept of Anxiety*, trans. Reidar Thomte (Princeton, N.J: Princeton University Press, 1980), p. 90.

[6] Søren Kierkegaard, *Samlede Vaerker*, Bd. 6 (København: Gyldendal, 1963), p. 179.

[7] William Faulkner, *The Sound and the Fury*, (New York: Vintage Books, 1929), p. 93.

[8] Faulkner, *The Sound and the Fury*, p. 216.

[9] William Faulkner, *As I Lay Dying*, (New York: Random House, 1964), p. 76.

[10] Kierkegaard, *The Concept of Anxiety*, p. 87.

[11] Translated: The "eye-glance".

[12] Faulkner, *As I Lay Dying*, pp. 163-164.

[13] Faulkner, *As I Lay Dying*, p. 167.

[14] Faulkner, *As I Lay Dying*, p. 196.

[15] Faulkner, As I Lay Dying, p. 166.

[16] Faulkner, As I Lay Dying, p. 115.

[17] Faulkner, As I Lay Dying, p. 95.

[18] Faulkner, As I Lay Dying, p. 244.

[19] Faulkner, As I Lay Dying, p. 139.

[20] Pär Lagerkvist, The Dwarf, trans. Alexandra Dick (New York: Hill and Wang, 1945), pp. 35-36.

[21] Lagerkvist, pp. 51-52.

[22] Lagerkvist, pp. 67-68.

[23] Lagerkvist, p. 198.

[24] Martin A. Hansen, Løgneren, (København: Gyldendal, 1950), pp. 155-156.

[25] Hansen, p. 182.

[26] Hansen, p. 186.

[27] Hansen, pp. 183-184.

[28] Hansen, pp. 92-93.

[29] Hansen, p. 81.

[30] Hansen, p. 169.

[31] Hansen, pp. 186-187.

CONCLUSION
THE POLITICAL EROS OF FORM AND BEAUTY

I have discussed Modernism as a product of a hermeneutical process whose aim it is to demystify reality and social relationships in order to create new meaning. The creation of meaning, and the creation of fictitious form and content is a dialectical process; there is a dialectical relationship between past and future, time and Eternity, "remembering backwards" and "remembering forward", separation and integration, negation and affirmation, and, finally, between unfreedom and freedom. I interpreted the novels, A Portrait, Ulysses, and Havoc as negative solutions to the apparently unresolvable fragmentation of social and psychological reality and to the apparently alienated existence of literary characters that were subjected to an oppressive and repressive social order; and I regarded Hunger, As I Lay Dying, The Dwarf, and The Liar as literary works that represent an affirmation through negation, through the cathartic purging of negative thoughts and emotions.

The division between the two types of novels I chose to analyze became clear when related to the philosophy of Søren Kierkegaard and Karl Marx, and to the metapsychology of Sigmund Freud; these varying philosophical systems seek to de-mystify "appearance" in order to re-create "essence". "Essence" is defined as the actual human dimension, the liberated human potential that becomes actual or real once the false nature of established social relationships has been recognized; essence, or spirit, is also the product of a synthesis between body and soul, in Kierkegaard's terminology, and a synthesis of reason and emotion. Reason and emotion play an equally important role in Kierkegaard's philosophy, as the purely analytical and critical function of the aesthetic consciousness becomes a prelude to and a prefiguration of the passion and the faith of the human self in the ethical and religious stages. The esthete's creation of a mythical reality which is, essentially, the producing of aesthetic form, previses the transcendental, the timeless dimension. Thus, the esthete's deception is, partly, self-seduction, in that the creation of myth reveals the underlying potential, the possibility of another, "unreal" existential mode. This mode is reshaped progressively in Kierkegaard's philosophy, and finally becomes the subjective absolute. This absolute affirmation of subjectivity is symptomatic of a new individual who is liberated from the pseudo-reality of the given social relationships. The art, the myth, and the form created by the poetic intellect of the esthete progresses dialectically from mere illusion to an actualized potential, to art's real dimension, and aesthetic form becomes a transhistorical expression of hitherto repressed human possibilities.

Marcuse interprets the reality and unreality of art as follows:

> ... the world of a work of art is "unreal" in the ordinary sense of this word: it is a fictitious reality. But it is "unreal" not because it is less, but because it is more as well as qualitatively "other" than the established reality. As fictitious world, as illusion (Schein), it contains more truth than does everyday reality. For the latter is mystified in its institutions and relationships, which make necessity into choice, and alienation into self-realization. Only in the "illusory world" do things appear as what they are and what they can be. By virtue of this truth which art alone can express in sensuous representation) the world is inverted - it is the given reality, the ordinary world which now appears as untrue, as false, as deceptive reality.[1]

The potential "other" of art is transhistorical; it can be defined as Kierkegaard's gentagelse, a disruption of the process of time, a revelation of the continuity and universality of human emotions. This revelation creates freedom, and the liberating process is inevitably political as well as psychological, for the aesthetic image of man is opposed to the function and character of man in the so-called real world. Man is suppressed in the real world, due to the oppressive nature of social and political institutions. Social domination has made man adapt to a perverted ideal of freedom, an ideal which is fundamentally materialistic; freedom, in the modern world, has become fragmented, and the current belief is that you can only become partly free, free within a limited field of action. The causes of this restricted freedom are interpreted to be cultural and existential fragmentation, separation, and alienation.

It is my contention that the fragmentation that is presented in <u>Ulysses</u>, for example, is an illusion; reality is not necessarily fragmented. Rather, oppression - which creates external and internal division - is the result of total domination, or, the domination of the totality of social, political, and cultural ideals and institutions. I see <u>Ulysses</u> as a mere reflection, a negative mimesis, of that which is, of the apparent fragmentation, instead of an affirmation of that which could be. Fragmentation is only the appearance of things and becomes in itself part of the political will to repress, the will to alienate and divide. The proposition that modern reality, modern civilization, is fragmented, is the product of incomplete perception and cognition; domination permeates the society from top to bottom, and the apparent complexity that creates lack of communication between individuals and their government is the by-product of an ideology promoted by an established political elite, whose nature is overtly Fascist, and propagated to sustain and perpetuate the prevailing class structure. Alienation is not endemic to our society; its causality is political.

The aesthetic form seeks to re-create the image of man as unalienated, as an integrated whole, and as a being who communicates with time and with timelessness. I regard <u>As I Lay Dying</u>, <u>The Dwarf</u>, and <u>The Liar</u> as examples of a dialectic between doubt and affirmation; doubt as to the value of art itself, and affirmation as the resurrection of art as the timeless human dimension. Creating a fictitious reality, in <u>The Liar</u>, becomes synonymous with creating reality, the reality of Eros, and the novel contradicts, in a way, the author's own doubt and skepticism as to the validity of fiction.

Darl's perception, in <u>As I Lay Dying</u>, that he is <u>are</u>, expresses the same validation, the resurrection of poetic vision as a second dimension, the other half of Darl's "are-ness". Totality and integration become the actual human dimension; fragmentation is appearance, <u>Schein</u>.

The aesthetic form which contains the category of the Beautiful, manifests an innate human quality: human sexuality and sensuousness; it operates under the law of the pleasure principle and evokes the image of past happiness, the image of the pre-Oedipal Eros. The erotic quality of Beauty, the pleasure principle, "rebels against the prevailing reality principle of domination".[2] Political Eros is the most sublimated form of aesthetic Beauty:

> In the creation of an aesthetic form, in which the horror of fascism continues to cry out in spite of all forces of repression and forgetting the life instincts rebel against the global sado-masochistic phase of contemporary civilization. The return of the repressed, achieved and preserved in the work of art, may intensify this rebellion.[3]

Aesthetic form is an expression of liberation, and Kierkegaard's esthete participates, through his senuousness and his myth-making faculty, in the process of liberation. The woman that he liberates and endows with Eros becomes his own self, and the dialectic between intellect and passion in *Diary of a Seducer* is a dialectic between two aspects of the self. The esthete recalls a moment of gratification and perpetuates it, and memory, as <u>gentagelse</u>, becomes the revolutionary instrument of aesthetic form; revolution becomes the telos of aesthetic form, as form recognizes "what is and what could be, within and beyond the social conditions".[4]

The political Eros of art, its liberation of the image of social and sexual unification, represents the future of human civilization, the utopian reality. Utopia, here, does not denote illusion, but self-realization. Fictitious reality does not exclude given reality, but includes it in order to negate it, de-mystify it, and re-create the larger reality of the self. Art negates non-being and creates being.

CONCLUSION REFERENCES

[1] Herbert Marcuse, The Aesthetic Dimension: Toward a Critique of Marxist Aesthetics (Boston: Beacon Press, 1978), p. 54.

[2] Marcuse, p. 62.

[3] Marcuse, p. 64.

[4] Marcuse, p. 67.

BIBLIOGRAPHY

Benjamin, Walter. "The Story Teller and Artisan Cultures." In Critical Sociology, Paul Connerton, ed. London: Hazell Watson & Viney Ltd., Aylesbury, Bucks, 1976.

Faulkner, William. As I Lay Dying. New York: Random House, 1964.

Faulkner, William. The Sound and the Fury. New York: Vintage Books, 1929.

Freud, Sigmund. Civilization and Its Discontents. New York: W.W. Norton & Company, 1962.

Freud, Sigmund. Complete Psychological Works, Vol. 18. London: The Hogarth Press, 1955.

Habermas, Jürgen. "Systematically Distorted Communication." In Critical Sociology, Paul Connerton, ed. London: Hazell Watson & Viney Ltd., Aylesbury, Bucks, 1976.

Hamsun, Knut. Hunger. Translated from the Norwegian by Robert Bly. New York: Farrar, Straus and Giroux, 1967.

Hansen, Martin A. Løgneren. København: Gyldendal, 1950.

Jameson, Fredric. Marxism and Form. Princeton, New Jersey: Princeton University Press, 1971.

Joyce, James. A Portrait of the Artist as a Young Man. New York: Penguin Books, 1976.

Joyce, James. Ulysses. London: The Bodley Head, 1960.

Kierkegaard, Søren. The Concept of Anxiety. Translated from the Danish by Reidar Thomte. Princeton, New Jersey: Princeton University Press, 1980.

Kierkegaard, Søren. Either-Or. Translated from the Danish by David F. Swenson and Lillian Marvin Swenson. Garden City, New York: Anchor Books, 1959.

Kierkegaard, Søren. Samlede Vaerker, Bd. 2. København: Gyldendal, 1963.

Kierkegaard, Søren. Samlede Vaerker, Bd. 5. København: Gyldendal, 1963.

Kierkegaard, Søren. Samlede Vaerker, Bd. 6. København: Gyldendal, 1963.

Kierkegaard, Søren. Samlede Vaerker, Bd. 7. København: Gyldendal, 1963.

Kierkegaard, Søren. Samlede Vaerker, Bd. 9. København: Gyldendal, 1963.

Kierkegaard, Søren. Samlede Vaerker, Bd. 10. København: Gyldendal, 1963.

Kristensen, Tom. Haervaerk. København: Gyldendal, 1930.

Lagerkvist, Pär. The Dwarf. Translated from the Swedish by Alexandra Dick. New York: Hill and Wang, 1945.

Lukacs, Georg. Kunst og kapitalisme. København: Nordisk Forlag, 1971.

Lukacs, Georg. The Meaning of Contemporary Realism. London: Merlin Press, 1962.

Marcuse, Herbert. The Aesthetic Dimension. Boston: Beacon Press, 1978.

Marcuse, Herbert. Eros and Civilization. Boston: Beacon Press, 1966.

Marx, Karl. Capital. Volume I. New York: International Publishers, 1967.

Ricoeur, Paul. Freud and Philosophy. New Haven: Yale University Press, 1970.

Ricoeur, Paul. "Hermeneutics: Restoration of Meaning or Reduction of Illusion?" In Critical Sociology, Paul Connerton, ed. London: Hazell Watson & Viney Ltd., Aylesbury, Bucks, 1976.

Marija Petrovska

MEROPE
The Dramatic Impact of a Myth

American University Studies: Series III, Comparative Literature. Vol. 9
ISBN 0-8204-0084-X   211 pp. pb./lam. US $ 18.95
recommended prices – alterations reserved

The legend of Merope, whose basic theme is maternal love, has enjoyed widespread popularity in the world of the theatre, though Euripides' tragedy *Chresphontes,* which dealt with this myth, is lost. Aristotle, in his *Poetics,* mentions the effectiveness of recognition as a means of astounding the listener: as the best example he points out the situation in the *Chresphontes,* when Merope, at the point of slaying her son, recognizes him in time. The popularity of the Merope legend began in Italy at the end of the 16th century, then migrated to France, where several 17th-century playwrights realized its appeal. In the 18th century, three famous authors produced their versions of the myth, namely Scipione Maffei, Voltaire and Vittorio Alfieri. Matthew Arnold's *Merope* is the best known English version, while the other 19th-century interpretations of the myth, produced in Italy, Germany, Portugal and Greece have fallen into oblivion.
Contents: The Italian Cinquecento – The French version of *Merope* before Voltaire – The versions by Maffei, Voltaire and Alfieri – *Merope* in England – Nineteenth-century versions.

PETER LANG PUBLISHING, INC.
34 East 39th Street
USA – New York, NY 10016

Steven E. Alford

IRONY AND THE LOGIC OF THE ROMANTIC IMAGINATION

American University Studies: Series III, Comparative Literature. Vol. 13
ISBN 0-8204-0110-2   184 pp. pb./lam. US $ 19.45
recommended prices – alterations reserved

This study examines romantic irony as a principle of style in the work of Friedrich Schlegel and William Blake. The first half traces Schlegel's critique of the principles of identity and noncontradiction, his development of a *romantic* logic, his view of dialectic and rhetoric, and how romantic irony is a stylistic mirror if the results of his critique of formal logic. These findings are tested in a close reading of his essay *Über die Unverständlichkeit* (1800). The second part examines the suggestive relation between Blake and Schlegel's views on logic, dialectic, and rhetoric, and uses these views as the basis for a reading of *The Marriage of Heaven and Hell* (1794). Both thinkers support the conclusion that romantic irony as a principle of style has two moments which can be characterized hermeneutically as negative dialectical and performative.

Contents: This study examines romantic irony as a principle of style in the work of Friedrich Schlegel and William Blake, using Schlegel's «Über die Unverständlichkeit» and Blake's «The Marriage of Heaven and Hell.»

PETER LANG PUBLISHING, INC.
34 East 39th Street
USA – New York, NY 10016